Martin Sheen

Actor and Activist

by Jim Hargrove

CHILDRENS PRESS ®

CHICAGO

PICTURE ACKNOWLEDGMENTS

AP/Wide World Photos—pages 8, 63 (bottom right), 64 (top right), 65 (bottom left), 67 (3 photos), 68

Photos Courtesy of Martin Sheen—pages 12, 36, 61 (3 photos), 62 (2 photos), 63 (top right), 64 (bottom left and right), 65 (top left and right), 66 (2 photos), 112

UPI/Bettmann Newsphotos—pages 2, 24, 63 (top left and bottom left), 64 (top left), 65 (bottom right)

Cover illustration by Len W. Meents

Library of Congress Cataloging-in-Publication Data

Hargrove, Jim.
    Martin Sheen: actor and activist / by Jim Hargrove.
        p.   cm.
    Includes index.
    Summary: Surveys the life and work of the actor, known
for such films as "Apocalypse Now."
    ISBN 0-516-03274-7
    1. Sheen, Martin—Juvenile literature. 2. Actors—United
States—Biography—Juvenile literature. 3. Political
activists—United States—Biography—Juvenile literature.
[1. Sheen, Martin. 2. Actors and actresses.] I. Title.
PN2287.S3715H37   1991
791.43'028'092—dc20
[B]   91-7793
                                                                         CIP
                                                                          AC

Table of Contents

In 1990 Martin Sheen and thirty-six others who were protesting in the rotunda of the Capitol in Washington, D.C., were arrested.

Chapter 1

THE TRESPASSING STAR

When he began looking for acting jobs in 1959, eighteen-year-old Ramon Estevez quickly discovered that he had a problem. His Spanish name made many show business people think that he should play only Hispanic roles. At the time, there were relatively few parts for Hispanics in American stage and screen productions.

It was an odd situation. Ramon was born in America and neither looked Spanish nor sounded Spanish when he spoke. His father had been born in Spain; his mother was Irish. Nevertheless, he realized that his name prevented him from being considered for many acting jobs.

Ramon decided to change his luck by changing his name. He started calling himself Martin Sheen. Gradually at first, he began finding work as an actor. Over the next three decades, Martin Sheen became one of the busiest and most successful actors in American show business.

Although he had already appeared in dozens of television programs and theatrical films, Sheen became a Hollywood superstar in 1979. That year, United Artists released *Apocalypse Now*, a movie about the Vietnam War. As the central character of the film, Martin Sheen appeared in nearly every scene. A small but important role in *Gandhi* and a major part in *That Championship Season*, both released in 1982, helped cement his grip on stardom.

During the 1980s, a development began to unfold that took the actor entirely by surprise. All of his four children began acting careers of their own, all four appearing in theatrical motion pictures as well as television productions. Two of his children, first-born son Emilio Estevez and third child Charlie Sheen, became superstars themselves.

All of this fame for one family might be enough to make a father think about retirement. But in the middle 1980s, just as his children were making their marks in motion pictures, Martin Sheen began doing a most curious thing. He began getting arrested, first in New York City, then in the Nevada desert, and then time and time again.

By late 1990, by his own count, Sheen had been arrested more than forty times. "I'm currently on a year's probation for a series of arrests," he said in October 1990. "They're over forty-one or forty-two now, but I've honestly lost count. I know it's in there someplace."

It should come as little surprise that Sheen has not been arrested for robbing banks. With a few loans from his sons, he could probably buy a bank or two. The legal charge made most often against him is trespassing.

At first glance, it may seem even more curious that his legal problems began soon after he renewed his faith in

Catholicism, the religion of his youth. But his spirituality is really the driving force behind his many arrests.

On October 25 and 26, 1990, shortly before leaving for Paris to film an HBO (Home Box Office) movie, Martin Sheen took part in an interview especially for this book. Much of the material presented in the pages that follow, and most of Sheen's words, were taken from that lengthy talk. During the discussion, Sheen's personal warmth, his love for his family and for his God, and his deep concern for his country came shining through.

Sheen spent much of his energy explaining how his Catholic faith and his legal problems sprang from the same source: a love of God and love for his fellow human beings. How a spiritual renewal led a movie star into difficulties with America's legal system is a story even more interesting than the latest box-office hit.

The tale begins in Dayton, Ohio. There, a young boy named Ramon Estevez dreamed of one day becoming a serious actor. As a youth, however, he spent most of his time in school and on a nearby golf course. If a stray golf ball with "Martin Sheen" printed on it had fallen at his feet, the youngster wouldn't have recognized the name at all.

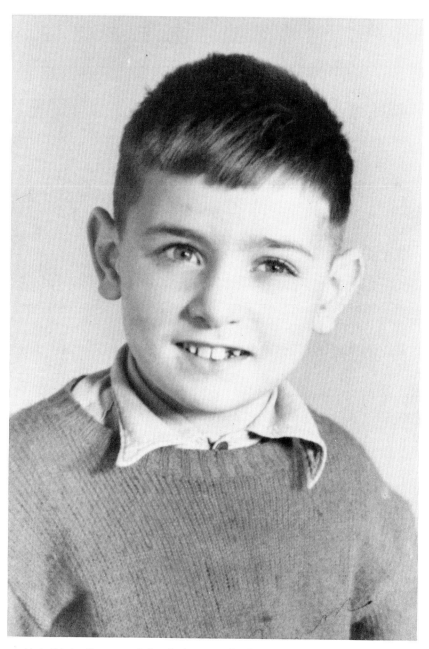

Holy Trinity Grammar School photograph of nine-year-old Ramon Estevez

Chapter 2

HOW THE OTHER HALF LIVED

If you had plenty of money and lived in Dayton, Ohio, in the 1950s, you were probably familiar with the Dayton Country Club. It was where many of the city's elite would meet. Among the private club's members were doctors, lawyers, business leaders—even people who were rich simply because their parents were rich.

The club's biggest attraction was its sprawling golf course. There, members and their guests could enjoy attempting the almost-impossible task of finishing 18 holes of golf in less than seventy-one golf strokes, par for the course.

Not everyone who walked up and down the hilly fairways was wealthy, however. Each summer, a group of about forty boys, mostly teenagers, worked at the club as caddies. Caddies carry golf bags filled with clubs and extra balls, leaving golfers free to walk along the fairways without shouldering a heavy load.

During most of the 1950s, one of the caddies at the Dayton Country Club was a Catholic school student named Ramon Estevez. In a few more years, the young man would adopt the stage name of Martin Sheen.

"I caddied from the time I was nine until I was eighteen,"

13

Sheen recalled, "and that meant that from the spring to the early fall I would be—most days—on the golf course." In 1949, the year he began caddying, caddies were paid $1.25 for carrying a set of clubs over the entire course. Considering the length of an average game, the payment amounted to about thirty cents an hour, not counting tips.

There was, however, a simple way to earn money faster. With just a bit of luck, a caddie could carry two sets of bags for two different players who were golfing in the same group. In 1949, payment for a "double" was $2.75, and took about the same amount of time. And, of course, there might be two tips instead of one. For youngsters like Ramon Estevez, however, carrying two sets of clubs up and down the hilly course was hard work.

The task was even harder for Ramon than for some of the other caddies his age. As Ramon Estevez, and even later as Martin Sheen, he was never very big. But he had a far more serious problem than his compact size.

"My left arm was smashed at the shoulder by forceps when I was born," he explained. "I was medically crippled." Although it isn't obvious in his movies, Martin Sheen's left arm is three inches shorter than his right, and practically useless. "It was a great deterrent," he continued about his youth, "but in the long run it turned out to be the fire that was lit under me, that moved me. It makes perfect sense when you think that sometimes the greatest Olympic champions were the ones that were crippled and had to fight back."

Caddying was harder work for Ramon than for most other boys. "You had two bags on your shoulder and you felt like you were going straight up a mountain," he said. But he did it for two reasons. First, he loved the game of golf, playing on most Mondays, which was always "caddie day" at the Dayton Golf Course. But the second reason was far more important. He badly needed the money his caddying brought in.

Ramon Estevez was born in Dayton on August 3, 1940. He was the seventh son of Francesco and Mary Ann Estevez, and the first to be born in America. Five of his older brothers were born in Bermuda and one in Ireland. He has one sister. His mother, Mary Ann, came from Ireland, where her family was always in danger because they fought in the Irish Republican Army. Francesco hailed from Spain, coming to the United States by way of a number of other countries. In America, he eventually got a job as a drill-press operator at Dayton's National Cash Register Company plant.

Following years of nurturing her children in the Catholic faith, Mary Ann died when Ramon was only eleven years old. Suddenly, it seemed almost impossible to hold the motherless family together. But the priests and the faithful of nearby Holy Trinity Church helped Francesco find a way to keep his children at home. All the brothers were able to continue their studies at the parochial school run by Holy Trinity, and later, at nearby Chaminade High School, a Catholic parochial school for boys.

All of the Estevez brothers worked as caddies from an early age. "I'm one of nine boys and all my brothers had caddied in front of me," Martin explained. "I'm the seventh son. So it was just a natural progression. They all started at the same age I had. They taught me how to do it."

Fortunately, the golf course was not far from the Estevez family home. The crowded home was a small, three-bedroom brick house at 751 Brown Street, not far from downtown Dayton. Getting to the golf course was relatively easy. "Sometimes you'd walk if you didn't have the bus fare," Sheen recalled. "Otherwise, there was a bus that ran right up from where we lived. We lived in an area called South Park, and the country club was in Oakwood, a very exclusive area."

The money Ramon and his brothers earned as caddies was very important to their educations. "We went to a Catholic grade school and an all-boys Catholic high school," he remembered, "so there had to be tuition paid and you had to buy your own books and your own clothes. A lot of it was saved through the summer. My dad would keep seperate envelopes for all of us in his drawer. We'd give him the bulk of what we would earn day by day and we would keep our own allowances. One summer, I remember, I had saved more than $400, and that was big money in those days. So that would last almost through the end of the off-season, through the winter. And then it would start to be all wasted by the spring or late winter, so Pop would have to give us allowances for lunch and carfare and so forth."

Their work as caddies made it possible for the Estevez brothers to pay for their own schooling. And that made it easier for their father to stretch his meager paycheck far enough to put decent food on the family's table. The caddying work also gave Ramon and his brothers a chance to observe how at least some of Dayton's wealthiest people behaved.

"I got a pretty good look as a child at how the better half lived," he said. "And I wasn't impressed with these people." Like most of the other caddies, Ramon realized that he was working as a servant for the golfers who hired him.

"People with servants tend to forget their presence because they don't recognize servants as people very often," he said, "certainly not as equals. They thought I was deaf or dumb or something. They'd say things in front of you that would be insulting anywhere else. They just ignored you. They didn't acknowledge your presence. They would curse, you know, they would use foul language, which I always found embarrassing as a child. I learned a lot of language on the golf course from the people I worked for.

"They kind of let their hair down," he continued, "and many of them were so corrupt and dishonest. They didn't realize how funny they were when they cheated on each other.

"You really understood somebody's character in two sets of circumstances: one where he played golf and one where he played cards, both of which I used to do. If someone cheated in either one, I took a very dim view of his character. Anyone would . . . because so much of that is honorable, you know? I became a pretty good judge of character on the golf course."

In the 1950s, fewer women had jobs than do today. Many depended entirely on their husbands to give them spending money. Perhaps that is why, around 1955, Ramon and some of the other caddies began to notice that some women golfers, and a few men as well, were failing to give them tips. For caddies working at low wages, tips were extremely important, and now they were sorely missed.

On a Tuesday morning in mid-summer 1955, Ramon Estevez decided to lead the other caddies in a strike for higher wages. That was one way, he reasoned, to make up for lost tips. "You could endure anything if you thought you were going to be compensated," he said about the strike. "There were a couple of clubs that paid a bit more than ours did, but they were farther away. The club we worked at was our choice because it was so close. It was less than four miles away."

While playing golf the day before on caddie day, Ramon talked to his fellow caddies about the possibility of a work stoppage. He planned to call the strike the very next day, Tuesday morning. Tuesday was ladies day at the golf course, and it was some of the women golfers who seemed most reluctant to tip.

"I wanted to call it out just as the women began to arrive," he said. "In other words, we would hold to the last minute. Just before the boat sailed, we would refuse to lift anchor. I understood something about labor relations at an early age. Anybody who works does."

Early Tuesday morning, Ramon Estevez stood up in front of the other caddies gathered in the clubhouse. He called for a strike, in other words, a complete refusal to work. Some of the other caddies seemed stunned that the 15-year-old labor leader was prepared to follow through with his threat. His brother Al and soon his brother Joe stepped up to stand at his side.

"I felt very defenseless, very vulnerable, frightened," he recalled. "I had taken a step and there really wasn't any retreating." Nevertheless, he knew what his next steps would be. "I led the lads up to the parking lot and sat down." About fifteen of the caddies, most of the ones present at that time, were gathered in the parking lot as women began arriving for the morning's first rounds of golf.

On other days, caddies would often meet cars as they

arrived in the parking lot. By helping golfers with their bags, shoes, and other pieces of equipment, the caddies hoped to earn bigger tips. "And so there was a distinct difference when nobody did that," Sheen said. "The ladies were struggling with their things out there, and nobody was going to their assistance."

One great obstacle stood between the strikers and a successful strike. In charge of all the caddies was the Dayton Country Club caddie master—a man to be reckoned with. He soon proved that he also knew a thing or two about labor relations.

The caddie master walked out to the parking lot to face the disgruntled workers. The conversation soon became a shouting match. As the lively conversations continued, the lady golfers hauled their own gear into the club house. There, they put on their shoes and prepared for the morning's golf round. Despite the hollering, no one seemed to take the strike very seriously.

"There was a lot of tongue in cheek about it," Sheen recalled thirty-five years later, "because some of the women would just come out and the caddie master would talk to the individuals, take them aside and talk to them. We gradually lost our ranks," One by one, the caddies left the strike to catch a "loop," a slang term for a round of golf.

Within a few minutes, many of the would-be strikers were already out on the golf course. Soon, the caddie master walked over to where Ramon and his two brothers were holding out. "I'm giving you guys one last chance," he warned. "Either you come back and work now or you're fired, and you'll have to get out of here because you are on private property!"

"I remember that was a very important issue," the actor recalled, "that we were on private property all of a sudden." Although they were frightened and angry, the three brothers held their ground. Ramon said they would not return to work unless they were given higher wages.

"We're not going to raise the fees," was the caddie master's blunt reply. A few more words were spoken, especially the words "private property," and eventually all three brothers were fired. Two other caddies who held on to the end were fired as well. No longer with jobs, and suddenly on very private property, the five boys began the long walk home.

"We went home," Sheen remembered, "and we talked about it and we waited to hear from friends to see what the reaction was. It wasn't very significant. People thought we were a bunch of fools and I was the chief fool. That was the feeling I got. And I felt like a fool because a few days later I went back. And I finished out the summer and I never called another strike. And the lads were good enough not to throw it up to me. They just never mentioned it."

Young Ramon Estevez was a very good golfer and, when not on strike, which was most of the time, he was a superb caddie. The Dayton Country Club caddie master was undoubtedly happy to see him return.

Even to this day, however, Martin Sheen the movie star looks back with a bit of sorrow on his short-lived strike. "I felt betrayed by a lot of the lads. We didn't stick together and I realized it wasn't well planned. One part of it that disappointed me was how they had gotten to the individuals. How the caddie master had gone and pulled aside the lads one at a time, two at a time, and talked to them without my being able to overhear. It was the same old story. I was told, 'You're a fool and you're going down the wrong road and you're going to get in trouble.'"

Ramon continued to work at the Dayton Country Club until he was eighteen years old. Near the end of his career as a caddie came one of the highlights of his youth.

In 1958, the U.S. Professional Golfers' Association held its championship series at the Miami Valley Country Club in Dayton. Golf officials scoured the city to find the best caddies to carry bags for the famous golfers who were taking part in the tournament. Among the lucky people selected were Ramon Estevez and eight or ten other caddies from the Dayton Country Club. Unfortunately, the professional that Ramon caddied for was cut after the first round. But another of the Dayton caddies worked for the golfer who eventually won the tournament. It was a great source of pride for all the caddies at the Dayton Country Club.

For Ramon, however, even that honor was not the highlight of the PGA championship that year. Among the professional golfers who came to Dayton in 1958 was a man named Ed Furgol. Furgol had won the U.S. Open golf tournament in 1954. He was a great golfer, made even greater by the fact that he had a withered left arm.

Even as a celebrity himself, Martin Sheen still recalled the handicapped golfer with awe. "I followed him around one day and watched him play. He was one of those spectacular athletes who had to overcome a defect. His left arm was about half as long as his right. And he won the U.S. Open! To watch him swing was a miraculous occasion. He would wrap the club literally around his neck on his backswing, so that it was all the way around his neck and on the other side of his body. He would whip it around like he was snapping a bull whip. And he was sensational. Ed Furgol was one of my heroes."

To a young caddie with a similar disability, Ed Furgol seemed to prove that almost anything was possible.

Martin Sheen and Al Pacino sit under a statue of Julius Caesar after they appeared in Shakespeare's *Julius Caesar* in 1988. The two actors met when they both worked at the Living Theater in New York City.

Chapter 3

THE RISING GENERATION

Ramon Estevez continued caddying throughout his high school career. But he was quickly developing some other interests as well. In his freshman year at the all-boys Chaminade High School, the students organized a teen club. Ramon was elected the club's first president.

During the same year, a young priest named Father Alfred Drapp arrived at Holy Trinity parish. The priest and the schoolboy became good friends. Eventually, Father Drapp played an important role in helping Ramon become an actor.

At Chaminade High School, Ramon's acting talents became apparent. During his earliest days there some students giggled at his habit of standing on wooden boxes to recite poetry. But by the time he reached his junior year he had appeared in more than a dozen school plays.

His first real break as an actor came when he was seventeen years old. The good luck came at a critical time. As he himself put it, "That was the summer I flunked out of high school." Ramon was attending summer school make-up classes when he auditioned for a local television program called *The Rising Generation*. "It was a very popular talent show on every Saturday night in Dayton," he said. "I would watch it all the time."

The skill Ramon Estevez wanted to showcase—acting—was different from the television program's normal fare. "I noticed that of all the talent they would have," he said, "singers and dancers and musicians and comics and magicians and so forth, they never had an actor."

Ramon went to the station's Dayton studio and auditioned for the show. He read a story written by an African-American minister who was skilled at dramatizing the Bible for his congregation. "He wrote this beautiful piece on Genesis called 'The Creation,'" Sheen remembered. "He fancied God as a very loving father, creating the world by throwing stars against blackness. God walked across the earth, and where his footsteps would fall would be valleys, and he could push up mountains. He used that kind of imagery."

Viewers of *The Rising Generation* had the opportunity to vote for their favorite performers. After watching the show on Saturday night, many people sent postcards to the station to cast their ballots. Ramon received the most votes for the week and was invited back for the finals, which were held every few months. The grand prize was an all expenses paid trip for two to New York City. Even more important for young performers like Ramon, the prize included a chance to audition at the CBS television network headquarters in New York.

Ramon won the grand prize and traveled to New York City with his older brother Manuel in September 1958. His first airplane flight, taken at a time when jets were already taking over the skies, was aboard a TWA propeller plane. For the five-day visit, the two brothers stayed at a Sheraton hotel in lower Manhattan. They spent much of their time visiting some of the many tourist attractions in New York City.

At the audition, Ramon met the casting director for CBS, a man named Robert Dale Martin. Martin was impressed by the young actor's beautiful baritone voice. "You can't do much acting in Dayton," he said to Ramon, "and so I think you ought to give New York some thought." Robert Martin urged the teenager to see him again if he decided to return to the city. "He was very encouraging to me," Sheen remembered about the CBS director. "He was a very good and decent man."

Soon after the audition, Ramon returned to Dayton. He attended high school classes briefly as a senior during the fall and winter of 1958. But he couldn't keep his mind on his studies. He had already decided to become an actor. He spent his few remaining months in Dayton dreaming of New York City.

Francesco, his father, was deeply disappointed when he learned about Ramon's decision. Francesco wanted his seventh son to attend college. Ramon deliberately flunked the entrance exam at the University of Dayton to avoid a confrontation with his father. In one of his greatest early performances, Ramon scored three out of a possible one hundred points on the exam, an all-time record low.

As the cold Ohio winter progressed, Ramon grew more and more anxious to move to New York. Unfortunately, he didn't have enough money to make the move possible. Considering that the teenager had not yet finished high school, it is perhaps surprising that Father Alfred Drapp decided to come to his rescue. "He gave me the money, he loaned it to me," Sheen remembered. "At that time it was a substantial sum, and it was given over a period of months. He sent me some more in New York to keep me going." The priest also talked to Francesco, somehow convincing the older man that the move to New York was in his son's best interests.

Ramon arrived back in New York City on February 1, 1959. On February 2, using part of Father Drapp's loan, he rented a tiny room in a boarding house at 131 East 30th Street in Manhattan. The next day, Buddy Holly died in an Iowa plane crash with two other rock music pioneers. In New York, Ramon quickly discovered that a Catholic church, St. Stephen's, was just a block or two away, on 28th Street. For the next few years, he regularly attended mass there.

It took Ramon only a few days to find a job, but not as an actor. He earned forty-two dollars a week as a night stock boy at the offices of American Express, the well-known credit card company. The salary made it barely possible to survive in a city as expensive as New York. Planning a monthly budget was particularly difficult. "I had it down to one week when I wouldn't do my laundry, or when I would cut down on milk," he said. Some days he would walk instead of ride on a bus or the subway. It was still years before he learned to drive a car. ("I didn't learn to drive until I was twenty-eight," he said. "I tried to learn when I was a kid, but I was hopeless.")

By working at night, he was free during the day to attend casting calls. During a casting call, producers of plays for the stage and sometimes even television and movies listen to actors read scripts. A few lucky actors and actresses are then selected for the stage or screen production.

It was during his first casting calls that Ramon Estevez decided to change his name. Because his real name was Spanish in origin, the young actor feared that he was being asked to try out only for Hispanic roles, which were limited. He had been born in the United States and he neither sounded nor looked Spanish. And so he chose Martin Sheen as his stage name—Martin from CBS's Robert Dale Martin and Sheen from Fulton J. Sheen, a well-known bishop in the Catholic church who often appeared on television.

From that point on, Ramon Estevez searched for acting jobs as Martin Sheen, even though he always liked his real name. "I never changed my name officially," he said in 1990.

"My name is still Ramon Estevez on my passport, my birth certificate, driver's license, everything, every official document. It's just a stage name."

As a teenaged actor available for work, Martin Sheen realized that he should be taking acting lessons, but he couldn't afford them. With a group of other young actors in similar need, he organized a performance company called the Actor's Co-Op, under the leadership of Vasek Simek. In a rented loft next to New York's old Madison Square Garden, the group performed highlights of well-known plays.

Another member of the Actor's Co-Op was a young, unknown actress named Barbra Streisand. "No one knew who she was," Sheen remembered many years later. "She didn't sing in the Actor's Co-Op. A couple of years later the same little girl from our group made it on Broadway in a show called *I Can Get It For You Wholesale*. That was her first big break."

During his brief stay at the Actor's Co-Op, Sheen met a man named John Evans. He was the nephew of a famous Englishwoman named Dame Edith Evans, and he was working with an off-Broadway theatrical group called the Living Theater, which was led by Julian Beck and Judith Malina. John Evans was about to begin acting in a Broadway play and was planning to leave the Living Theater. He suggested that Martin Sheen might take his place.

"It turned out he was a curtain-puller and worked with

props," Sheen discovered. "He was a general backstage handyman. And that's how I started working at the Living Theater." Sheen must have been discouraged that his first work in the Living Theater involved raising and lowering the curtain. With another young actor named Al Pacino, Sheen moved props, painted scenery, cleaned the toilets, raised and lowered the curtain, and generally made himself useful. By the end of 1960, he was janitor for the entire building that housed the Living Theater.

Performing janitorial services and working with props was not Martin Sheen's career goal. His first little break came soon enough. "You can't stay in the theater long before you start acting," he said. "I mean, no one in the theater is there to do props. Most people, at least all of the actors, are there to do performances. I just looked for an opportunity. They had these Monday night programs when the theater was dark and they presented a series of three one-act plays. One of them was *Purgatory* [by William Butler Yeats] and they asked me if I'd play the son and I said 'delighted,' and that was the first time I got paid for acting. I got paid five dollars a performance and we did four performances on four successive Monday nights."

Theater people work at night, and those demands made it impossible for Sheen to hold onto his job at American Express. Around the time he became a professional actor, real poverty began to take hold.

New York City was, and still is, famous for its fine restaurants. For his dining pleasure, Martin Sheen often visited the Salvation Army, where breakfast was fifteen cents and dinner was only a nickel more. The few times he was unable to come up with the money, a meal was never refused.

In December 1960, while Sheen was working at the Living Theater, he met a young woman named Janet Templeton. Considering the nature of his first meetings with her, it is remarkable that Janet eventually became his wife, the mother of his four children, and his life-long companion.

"We had a mutual friend who was a stage manager at the Living Theater," Sheen said. "Janet, my wife, was an art student who was on a scholarship at the New School for Social Research on Sixth Avenue and Twelfth Street. So we were just two blocks apart. . . . He had a little Vespa motor scooter and he took me up to her house on 42nd Street and he gave me a painting that she had done and had given to him to keep for her because she had no locker or no room in her locker."

During the short scooter trip uptown, Sheen's friend made up a story that would give Martin an excuse to talk to Janet. "Well," the friend shouted, inventing a story about the painting, "I'll tell her it's become lost and you found it."

It wasn't much of a plan, but as Sheen said later, "I didn't question this at the time. I just wanted to meet her."

When the two young men arrived at 42nd Street, Sheen

walked up to the door and presented the painting to Janet, speaking the immortal words, "Here, I found this."

"She knew I was a fool," he admitted. That opinion lasted for some time. Although he worked six nights a week at the theater, the actor took every opportunity he could find to see the young woman. "I was really intrigued with her, obviously, right from the start," he said. "And I just pursued her. I was relentless with her. I just wore down her resistance and eventually I moved in."

Since Sheen worked during the evenings, it was difficult for the young couple to enjoy nights out together at restaurants and shows. Perhaps it was just as well.

Whenever it was necessary, Martin continued eating meals at the Salvation Army. Through some actors at the Living Theater, however, he was introduced to a group of politically active people who performed services at an organization called the Catholic Worker. Dedicated to assisting poor and politically powerless people, the Catholic Worker always had plenty of odd jobs available for volunteers. Even more important to a hungry young actor, the organization offered free hot meals. Sheen quickly decided that the Catholic Worker chef was a bit more refined than the cooks at the Salvation Army. "It was the only place I knew of in New York where you could eat a very decent hot meal every night and not have to pay for it nor listen to anyone's sermon," he said about the Catholic Worker.

Soon after Martin moved into Janet's Manhattan apartment, both were thrown out. The landlord considered it a sin for two unmarried people to live together. For the better part of the next decade, they moved many times, usually to a less expensive apartment. It was during this impoverished period that Martin Sheen learned his trade as an actor.

One of the most successful plays staged by the Living Theater was called *The Connection*. The play examined the nature of drug abuse, a common problem now but still a shocking subject in the early 1960s. During the production's long run, Sheen replaced another actor in the important role of Ernie.

In *The Connection*, Sheen's character Ernie was a villainous junkie who waited with a group of other addicts for the arrival of a package of heroin. While they waited, the junkies downplayed the seriousness of their problems. When the package finally arrived, one of the addicts died from an overdose. During performances of the play, members of the audience often fainted as the death scene unfolded with horrifying realism.

In the summer of 1961, the Living Theater became the official representative of the United States at the Theater of Nations Festival in Paris. Janet traveled to Europe with Martin and the rest of the Living Theater company.

Like the volunteers at the Catholic Worker, many of the actors in the Living Theater hoped to change a number of aspects of American life. The Living Theater was an early supporter of a movement called Ban the Bomb. People in this movement felt that the growing number of nuclear weapons throughout the world was dangerous. They asked people of all nations, and the United States in particular, to stop their governments from stockpiling weapons. The movement gave Martin Sheen his first exposure to political activism.

By the time the Living Theater returned to the United States, Martin and Janet had decided to get married. They were wed on December 23, 1961, at St. Stephen's Church in Manhattan. At the time they could hardly have realized that they were starting a family that would eventually include five successful actors.

Patricia Neal and Martin Sheen appeared in a 1968 film of *The Subject Was Roses*. The stage version was Martin's first big hit.

Chapter 4

STAR MAKING

Martin Sheen made his television acting debut late in 1961, around the time he married Janet. He tried out for and won a small role as a villain in an episode of a series called *The Defenders*. At the time, it was one of only two dramatic television shows made in New York City. Most of the others were filmed in and around Los Angeles.

Aired on the CBS television network from 1961 until 1965, *The Defenders* starred E.G. Marshall and Robert Reed as father-and-son lawyers. The show received high praise from critics, including the *New York Times* television analyst Les Brown. "The series outshone most others on the networks for the quality of writing and acting and for its straightforward treatment of serious themes," Brown wrote.

Martin Sheen should have enjoyed his television debut. Unfortunately, he was so scared appearing before cameras for the first time that he remembered little about the filming. "Oh, I was shaking," he said. "My heart pounded and the blood rushed to my head. I have very little memory of exactly what went on. I have a scar on my leg where I fell down a fire escape during the filming of one scene. It's still on my leg and reminds me of that show."

He does recall that the episode was directed by Franklin J. Schaffner, a well-known television director who went on to direct a number of motion pictures, including *Patton*. For many years, Schaffner was the president of the Screen Directors Guild.

On May 12, 1962, Janet gave birth to the couple's first child, Emilio. "When Emilio was born, I tried to get into the delivery room with Janet," Martin said, "but they wouldn't let me in. I hadn't studied." Many New York doctors were willing to let husbands stand by their wives during labor, but only if the husbands attended special childbirthing classes. Martin had not, and was therefore barred from the delivery room.

In 1963, Sheen made a guest appearance on an episode of another highly regarded television show, *East Side, West Side*. The series starred George C. Scott, who soon went on to an illustrious career in movies. Scott and Sheen became good friends, and Scott clearly remembered their first show. Sheen played a drunk who abused his wife, and Scott marveled at how such a gentle man could suddenly turn into a hate-filled maniac when the cameras began to roll.

Later that same year, Martin Sheen was involved in one of the most foolish acts of his life. Janet was expecting her second child. Angered that he had not been allowed to attend the birth of Emilio, Martin decided to assist in the delivery of his new baby himself. Although he had never even seen a child being born, he decided to have no one else present to help Janet. He played the dual role of doctor and nurse in the living room of the family's little Staten Island apartment.

Janet went into labor and gave birth to Ramon Estevez on August 3, 1963. "Janet and I were there like a couple of animals," he confessed. "All we had was a bottle of alcohol and the *New York Times.*" As Ramon was being born, the husband helped his wife as best he could. But his lack of experience soon led to panic.

"I was so ignorant of what to expect," he said, "that after he was born I thought Janet was having his twin. That was the afterbirth and the placenta. I didn't have any idea what that was." Fearing that his wife might bleed to death, Martin called an ambulance.

By the time the medics arrived, the worst was over. Mother and child were already at rest. An attendant cut and tied the baby's umbilical cord and took the shaken family to a hospital. All, including the embarrassed father, were pronounced healthy and happy.

Four days later, on August 7, 1963, First Lady Jacqueline Kennedy, wife of President John F. Kennedy, gave birth to a baby boy named Patrick. As soon as the child was born at Otis Air Force Base on Cape Cod, doctors realized he had serious lung problems. The infant was rushed to a Boston hospital, where he died the following day. Americans, including Martin and Janet, mourned the child's death.

The actor saw great irony in the tragedy. Ramon, born to foolishly unprepared parents, grew up strong and healthy. But all the tools of modern medicine could not save the life of young Patrick Kennedy. Nor were they of much help 108 days later when, on November 22, 1963, the president himself died from an assassin's bullet.

Far happier news was made in 1964. That year, Martin Sheen made his Broadway debut in a play called *Never Live Over a Pretzel Factory*. That show had a brief run and is largely forgotten now. Later in the year, however, Martin landed a much more significant role. In his second Broadway play, *The Subject Was Roses*, Sheen portrayed a young soldier who returns home and must try to cope with his quarreling parents. The drama won a Pulitzer Prize for author Frank Gilroy, and Sheen was nominated for a Tony Award, the Broadway equivalent of an Oscar.

It was high praise for an actor still in his middle twenties, even though on award night Sheen lost out to the actor who played his father. In the long run, though, it was just as well. Throughout the rest of his career, Sheen consistently asked that his name be removed from lists of nominees for acting awards. He simply felt that those kinds of competitions were foolish.

During the long run of *The Subject Was Roses*, the American civil rights movement was in full swing. Leaders such as Dr. Martin Luther King, Jr. were in the forefront of a crusade for racial equality in the United States.

Martin Sheen was greatly moved by the impassioned pleas of Dr. King and other civil rights pioneers. While appearing in *The Subject Was Roses*, Martin talked to the general manager of the Broadway theater that was presenting the play. He said that he and some other actors could put on a benefit performance to raise money for the civil rights movement. The manager agreed to the plan, but pointed out that they probably wouldn't take in much money.

Soon after the talk, Sheen walked across Broadway to another theater, where Sammy Davis, Jr. was appearing in *Golden Boy*. Davis quickly agreed to help. Next, Sheen walked a few hundred yards up Broadway to where Barbra Streisand was starring in *Funny Girl*. She too agreed to appear in the benefit. Many other Broadway performers followed, and the resulting show was a smashing success.

On the night of the benefit, Dr. Martin Luther King, Jr. appeared at the theater. He eventually went backstage to greet the performers. Sheen was thrilled that he was about to meet the famous civil rights leader. But it wasn't to happen. "I was stuck between these two people and he walked right by me," he told a reporter for *Rolling Stone* magazine. "I never got to meet him."

Despite his success on Broadway, Martin Sheen had more and more reasons to try to keep his career moving along in the fast lane. On September 3, 1965, Janet gave birth to their third son, Carlos, who is now known to millions of movie fans as Charlie Sheen. About two years later, the family was made complete when, in 1967, Martin and Janet's youngest child and only daughter Renee was born. There was only limited time for the proud father to relax with his growing family.

It may seem hard to believe that the star of a successful Broadway play could have serious financial problems, but Martin Sheen did. "As long as we lived in New York," he said, "those ten years from 1959 to 1969, there was never a period of relative financial security. Never! All my children were born in New York from 1962 to 1967. It was a heavy expense."

To feed the growing number of kids at home, Sheen got as many television guest spots as he could. He played mostly forgettable roles in series such as *Medical Center*, *The Mod Squad*, *Route 66*, *The F.B.I.*, *My Three Sons*, and *Outer Limits*. For months before and after Renee was born, he had a continuing role in a daytime soap opera called *As the World Turns*.

"A lot of those shows were trash, frankly," Sheen said. "I played badly. They were produced badly. They had nothing to offer. They just filled up the airwaves and kept food in the icebox." A number of people involved in those television shows recalled that he sometimes brought his young children with him to the set.

In that same year, 1967, Martin got his first role in a theatrical motion picture. In *The Incident* he and fellow actor Tony Musante played a couple of New York toughs who bullied subway passengers. The movie isn't often shown today, but it provided the break Sheen needed to get started in motion pictures.

Soon after he completed *The Incident*, Sheen was hired to recreate his stage role in *The Subject Was Roses*. When the film was released in 1968, some critics complained that it lacked the full power of the Broadway production. But even the most sour reviewers had to admit that there was much that was good about the movie.

On the other hand, there were a number of things that were bad about New York City, at least as a place to raise children. In 1968, the same year the *The Subject Was Roses* was released, six-year-old Emilio Estevez was robbed at knife-point in the lobby of his family's apartment house. His twelve-year-old attacker made off with only twenty-six cents. But the incident convinced Martin and Janet that it was time to consider moving.

An ideal opportunity arose the following year. Director Mike Nichols was preparing to shoot a big, expensive movie based on the antiwar novel *Catch-22* by Joseph Heller. Director Nichols was on a roll, having recently completed an enormously popular movie called *The Graduate*. For his new production, money seemed to be no object. Among the many stars signed for *Catch-22* were Alan Arkin, Martin Balsam, Richard Benjamin, Art Garfunkel, Jack Gilford, Bob Newhart, Anthony Perkins, Paula Prentiss, Jon Voight, Orson Welles, and, of course, Martin Sheen. Filming was scheduled to begin in Mexico, move on to Los Angeles, and continue in Rome.

Martin, Janet, and their children arrived in Mexico in January 1969. "We were in Mexico for a couple of months and then we came up to Los Angeles and rented a house," Sheen recalled. "And I just decided not to live in New York again." Although they moved several times, Martin and Janet have lived in the Los Angeles area ever since.

While *Catch-22* was being shot in Mexico, most of the movie people stayed at the elegant Playa de Cortes Hotel in the resort town of Guaymas. Located along the beaches of the Gulf of California, the luxury hotels of Guaymas catered to wealthy vacationers, many of whom were Americans. Not far to the east, however, the Mexican residents of the town lived in far less lavish circumstances.

Many of the actors and other production people working on *Catch-22* were surprised when the Sheen family did not rent rooms in the Playa de Cortes Hotel. Instead, they took up residence in a little duplex apartment on the outskirts of the town's poorest neighborhood. Over the years, the reasons for this have been oddly distorted in a number of books and magazine articles.

Several writers reported that Sheen chose to live among the poorer Mexican citizens as a demonstration of friendship and concern for their living conditions. Sheen offers a simpler explanation for why he and his family didn't live in the hotel.

"It was just financial," he said. "We couldn't afford it. It was very expensive and we were on a limited budget, of course, so we were trying to save as much as we could. We rented a house in a little area called San Bernardo. There were a lot of Americans there, actually, because Guaymas was one of the tracking stations for the space shots for NASA. There were these new areas being developed, and we were able to get a duplex apartment in an area with a lot of other Americans."

His own part-Hispanic heritage left little room for Sheen to feel prejudiced against Mexicans. "We certainly were very close to a lot of the people from that community," he remembered. "They were in our house every night and our kids were in theirs."

By the time Martin had finished shooting his scenes in *Catch-22*, the Sheen family was settled in California. They didn't bother to bring their furniture from New York. "I left a friend to look after it," Sheen explained, "to sell what was worthy and to just give away what wasn't."

Just as his family was getting used to their new West Coast surroundings, Martin Sheen landed another job—in New York. His friend George C. Scott asked him to hurry eastward to appear in an off-broadway production of a drama by a South African playwright. For a little longer than a month, Sheen played the role of an Afrikaner in the dramatic play *Hello and Goodbye*. Colleen Dewhurst played his sister.

When he returned to the West Coast, the father found that his children were having little difficulty adapting to the California life-style. At just about the time of the move west, seven-year-old Emilio began writing short stories and poems. By the time he was eight, he had completed a handwritten teleplay for a then-popular television show, Rod Serling's *Night Gallery*. The script, written in pencil, was good enough to earn an official rejection slip from the program's producers.

Of the Sheens' three boys, Ramon, just a year younger than Emilio, was beginning to show signs that he would become the most shy and artistic. Youngest son Carlos was just the opposite, already a loud and rambunctious five-year-old beginning to take an interest in sports. Little Renee was still a toddler when the family resettled in California.

Because of Martin's successful acting roles, the Sheen family was no longer poor. Still, life in their new California neighborhood was expensive. Martin had to work constantly to pay the bills.

During 1969 and the early 1970s, Sheen appeared in a number of made-for-television movies, often billed as "Movies of the Week." Among them were *Then Came Bronson* (1969), *Goodbye, Raggedy Ann* and *Mongo's Back in Town* (both aired in 1971), and *Welcome Home, Johnny Bristol* and *Pursuit* (1972).

The most memorable of his early television movies also was produced and aired in 1972. In *That Certain Summer*, Sheen and fellow actor Hal Holbrook starred as a pair of homosexual men struggling for happiness in a hostile world. For his performance, Sheen was nominated for an Emmy Award. As soon as he learned about the nomination, however, he asked that his name be removed from the list.

For Martin Sheen, 1972 was a particularly busy year. Among the theatrical motion pictures released that year that he appeared in were *No Drums, No Bugles, Pickup on 101*, and George C. Scott's *Rage*.

Despite all those other roles, however, his most notable performance of 1972 was in a movie not released until two years later. *Badlands*, directed by Terrence Malick, was based on a true story about a teenaged boy and girl who went on a crime and murder spree in Nebraska in 1958. Sheen and a virtually unknown actress named Sissy Spacek starred as the mad lovers.

Probably because of its depressing subject matter, the film did not do particularly well at the box offices when it opened in 1974. But in the years that followed, it attained a kind of cult status on television and in videotape rental stores. Sheen always regarded his portrayal of Kit in *Badlands* as one of his finest performances, and many critics agreed. In recent years, however, he has been wary of playing such violent roles.

Without question, Martin Sheen was one of the busiest actors in Hollywood in 1972, active in both television and motion pictures. "I was doing television right up until the start of *Badlands*," he said, "and started doing it again right at the end of it, right after I finished shooting. [Director] Terry Malick was amazed at that."

Life in Hollywood's fast lane had its rewards, both artistically and financially. But Sheen soon discovered that it was filled with danger as well.

Chapter 5

THAT DARK NIGHT OF THE SOUL

By the early 1970s, Martin, Janet, and their four children were living on a little rented farm along the Pacific Coast Highway west of Los Angeles. "At that time the area was so rural it was much cheaper," he said. "You could get more for your money, get a few acres and a bigger house, which was what we needed with the kids." By 1974, the family had moved into the same Malibu home that Martin and Janet still live in today.

Throughout the early 1970s, Sheen moved quickly from one acting assignment to another. Jobs would frequently take him far from home. Janet and the four kids often accompanied him to distant places, locations that had been selected for his newest film projects.

In 1973, the Sheens went to Ireland, where Martin was working on a television movie called *Catholics*. The telefilm was being made for a highly respected series called *Playhouse 90*. But the Sheen children always remembered the trip for the present Martin gave them.

About thirteen years later, in 1986, Charlie Sheen recalled the occasion in a press release for one of his own movies. He remembered that his father "bought us a Super 8 movie camera, and we started putting together some stories." The father got the inexpensive camera hoping it would amuse his children while he was working. At the time, he had little idea what he had started.

Over the next few years, Emilio and Charlie used the camera to make amateur movies, complete with real-life movie stars. As luck would have it, the Sheen's Malibu neighborhood was home to a number of children who soon grew up to become Hollywood superstars.

"I have films to this day," Charlie continued, "with people like Sean Penn, Chris Penn, Rob and Chad Lowe, and Diane Lane in the cast, movies that range from violent police dramas to ridiculous comedies. We went into every aspect: writing, directing, acting, cinematography." About two years after getting their first cameras, the brothers moved up to sound equipment.

By 1974, Martin Sheen was working on one of his most famous television specials, *The Execution of Private Slovik*. The movie recreated the sad story about an American soldier who was shot for desertion. Sheen play the doomed serviceman.

"Slovik was given a batch of letters on the very morning he was shot," the actor said. "The mail had backed up for some months. So there were many letters that he'd never seen. In fact, he didn't read them all. He only read a few that morning. He couldn't get through them.

"Janet wrote to me a whole batch of letters and asked me not to open them until that scene was shot," Sheen continued. "And that's exactly what I did. One of them was so powerful that it just overwhelmed me. On camera I read it."

Since the letter was not historically accurate, it could not be used in the final version of the movie. But Sheen never forgot how moved he was by his wife's dramatic effort. It helped him to find the deep emotions he needed to portray the young soldier's final day.

The Execution of Private Slovik is notable for one other reason. At the age of nine, Carlos made his professional acting debut. His tiny part as an extra with a ten-second close-up could hardly be compared to his father's starring role. But perhaps it gave him some lasting memories. It was nine years before he had another professional role.

On December 18, 1974, the American Broadcasting Company aired one of the most famous television movies of all time, *The Missiles of October*. That landmark program retold a historic event in American history: the 1962 Cuban missile crisis.

In 1962, President John Kennedy learned that Russian soldiers were bringing guided missiles to the island of Cuba. It was a great danger to the United States because, for the first time, weapons capable of carrying nuclear bombs were within easy reach of American cities.

In *The Missiles of October*, William Devane played President Kennedy. Martin Sheen portrayed the president's brother, Attorney General Robert Kennedy. In the movie, as in real life, Robert was influential in shaping United States policy. He helped the president and the president's cabinet find a way to solve the crisis—and get rid of the missiles—without starting a war.

Both John Kennedy and his brother Robert were murdered in the 1960s. But other members of the Kennedy family, including Jacqueline, the president's widow, watched the film. All were impressed by the show's accuracy, as well as by the fine performance by Martin Sheen.

In 1975 and early 1976, Sheen worked in a number of television movies as well as on the live stage. From his work on screen, it was almost impossible to tell that trouble was brewing. But by now, the successes he had enjoyed in television shows and motion pictures were beginning to take a toll on his personal life.

Some years earlier, Sheen had abandoned the Catholic church. Although he still considered himself a Christian, he felt that he was simply too busy to attend mass. A moderate drinker in his youth, he began abusing alcohol badly. He started smoking more cigarettes than ever before.

"I was really fragmented," he admitted much later. "That was a term I used a lot. I was smoking and trying to work out. I was a contradiction. I was interested in spirituality and I was interested in the flesh. I was drinking heavily. I was angry about a lot of things. I was disappointed in myself and my career, my personal life. I was fragmented. I was just not whole, not healthy on any level. I was miserable to live with."

It was during the early stages of this crisis that Martin Sheen landed the biggest and toughest role of his life.

Early in 1976, director Francis Ford Coppola was returning to California from a trip to the Philippines. On those distant Pacific Islands, he was preparing to make a motion picture about the Vietnam War. At the time, Martin, Janet, and their four children were in Rome, where Martin was working on a motion picture called *The Cassandra Crossing*. In a series of hasty telephone calls, the actor was asked to fly to Los Angeles to meet Coppola. Sheen agreed, and the two men met for ten minutes at Los Angeles International Airport. The next day, Coppola offered him the part.

For some months, the director had been trying to find the right person to play the starring role in *Apocalypse Now*, his new film. Jack Nicholson wanted it, but was already under contract for another film. Steve McQueen and Al Pacino turned it down.

Sheen quickly accepted. On Easter Sunday, he flew back to Europe, where he wrapped up *The Cassandra Crossing* on Monday. By Tuesday, Janet and the children were on their way to California and Martin was flying to the Philippines.

All the principal players were finally in place for one of the most difficult shoots in the history of movies. "It was a watershed of my life," Sheen said, "both professionally and certainly spiritually."

In many ways, the jungles and rivers of the Philippine Islands look much like Vietnam. The Vietnam War had ended less than a year before filming began on *Apocalypse Now*. At the time, the Communist government of Vietnam was hardly ready to welcome an American film crew. The Philippines, therefore, was a logical place to shoot the movie.

Janet and the four kids flew to Manila, the capital of the islands, and soon followed Martin around the far-flung locations for the movie. Even in early spring, the Philippines were extremely hot and humid. Battle scenes required plenty of explosions. The smoke hung like a deathly fog in the sweltering air. Actors and crew members alike had trouble breathing. A number of people collapsed from heat exhaustion. Many scenes were shot at night, upsetting all plans for normal sleep. Through it all, director Coppola continuously rewrote the script, requiring new lines to be learned and existing scenes to be reshot.

The central character of *Apocalypse Now* is U.S. Special Services soldier named Captain Willard, played by Sheen. In the movie, Captain Willard is assigned to find, and kill, a renegade U.S. Army Green Berets officer named Kurtz, played by Marlon Brando.

In mid-May 1976, less than two months into the filming, Typhoon Olga hit the Philippines. The storm dropped more than three feet of rain during a six-day deluge. All of the movie's outdoor sets were destroyed. Production stopped for two months while the displays were rebuilt.

Many of the cast members decided to go home. Martin, Janet, and the four kids returned to Malibu. In the comfort of his house, the actor realized that he didn't want to go back to the Philippines. He demanded more money to complete the film, but Coppola refused. "Francis had to really, really wrangle with me and negotiate to get me to do anything," Sheen remembered. "I didn't trust anybody."

When it was finally time to go back to the set, the actor was filled with dread. He feared that he would not live to see the film completed. At the height of summer, when he returned to the draining heat of the Philippines, he began to take steps he hoped would keep him alive.

Much of *Apocalypse Now* takes place on a small patrol boat. The boat carries Captain Willard, Sheen's character, up a river to the jungle hideout of Colonel Kurtz.

"I couldn't swim and, look, we were spending all that time on the boat," Sheen explained. "I was very concerned about that. After this terrible storm came and ended shooting for a while, we came back for a few weeks to regroup and I took swimming lessons. I was concerned about surviving."

As the grueling shooting schedule continued, Emilio, Ramon, Charlie, and Renee all got to learn a great deal about life in the Philippines. Neither Martin nor Janet was aware that Emilio, at the age of fourteen, had begun drinking beer and hanging out in disreputable Filipino bars.

Although he was barely a teenager, Emilio soon realized that he was heading in a dangerous direction. He was desperately unhappy and homesick. His entire family was in the dense jungle of the Philippines, and he longed for the sunny beaches of Malibu. For week after week, he asked his father when they might go home. In a 1979 press release, Martin Sheen described how he and eldest son Emilio argued.

"I'd been telling him for six months," the father explained, "that we would be getting out of the jungle and going home—I knew that we couldn't, really. And he finally called me a liar. He was furious. . . . We were screaming at each other, just about ready to go at it, when Marlon [Brando] strolled by. He'd heard all the noise. He was acting as if he was just walking by but I'm sure he came to make sure we didn't get in a fight."

Martin and Janet understood that something needed to be done. Emilio, along with middle brother Ramon, were both sent home to Malibu. Charlie and Renee stayed on in the Philippines for a while longer.

For most of 1976 and the early months of 1977, Martin Sheen had terrible dreams about his work in the Philippines. His mental condition was worsened by his physical habits. He paid little attention to his diet, eating junk food by the ton without gaining weight. He smoked as many as three packs of cigarettes a day. As the star of *Apocalypse Now*, he was in nearly every scene of the movie. The schedule was grueling for everyone, but especially tough for him.

On Saturday, March 5, 1977, he suffered a heart attack and a nervous breakdown simultaneously. Janet had gone to Manila, and so he was alone in his room. He had suffered from chest pains the evening before. Soon after dawn, he was unable to stand up. Crawling on his hands and knees out of his room and to the side of the road, he eventually found his way to the film company's wardrobe van. Whisked to a temporary film office, the actor realized that he could die at any moment.

"Get me a priest," he said to the first doctor who examined him. When the clergyman arrived, he gave Sheen the last rites, a ceremony given to Catholics who are about to die. As part of those last rites, Martin confessed his sins. Unfortunately, the Filipino priest who listened to him did not speak English.

Several hours later, he was carried by helicopter to Manila, where Janet met him in the intensive care unit of the hospital. Even under skilled medical care, Sheen wept uncontrollably for hours. His stubbly beard, skin, and hair turned completely gray.

For weeks, Janet stayed by his side, often sleeping on the floor beside his bed. She made arrangements with a therapist in New York City to talk to Martin for hours over the telephone. While the Manila doctors treated his heart, Janet and the therapist nursed his spirits back to health—at least temporarily.

After about six weeks, Sheen was finally well enough to return to work. Unfortunately, work was becoming an endless nightmare. For months, Francis Ford Coppola had been struggling with his own demons to complete *Apocalypse Now*. The production was already late and far, far over budget. Sheen's illness seemed to bring Coppola back to his senses. Filming was completed in eight weeks.

Apocalypse Now opened in 1979 to wildly mixed critical reviews. Although most critics applauded the film's dazzling war scenes, many failed to understand some basic elements of the plot, especially the disturbing ending. Despite some complaints by critics, however, millions of people flocked to theaters to see *Apocalypse Now*. It received nine Academy Award nominations, although the list was quickly reduced to eight. Martin Sheen asked for his best actor nomination to be withdrawn.

The Vietnam War was over, and the most expensive movie

ever made about it was over as well. But for Martin Sheen, the war dragged on. For a period of about three years after he finished *Apocalypse Now*, the actor was at war with himself.

In 1990, Sheen explained how, in the years following *Apocalypse Now*, he felt just like the confused central character of the movie, a soldier ordered to kill a fellow American soldier. "If you wanted to know what it was like or who I was at that time," he said, "it's on the screen. I was that person. I was a terribly unhappy man, going through a lot of horrible things."

Alcohol played a major role in Sheen's problems. He drank heavily throughout much of the period. On two occasions he lived apart from Janet and his children for several months. At least once he wandered down a city street asking strangers if they believed in God. One night he got drunk in a San Francisco restaurant and noticed that his wallet, which contained several thousand dollars in cash, was missing. He created such a scene that the police were called. When they arrived, he tried to punch one of them. He spent several hours in jail.

Right after his collapse in 1977, Sheen had decided to change his ways. "My near-death experience made me frightened and I realized that I was lacking," he said thirteen years later, "and I wanted to get back to the church. And I did go back, but for a very short time, because I was really coming back out of fear. I was afraid that God would smite me for my sins. That lasted a very short period of time, and so I continued my journey for another four years."

Only years later did Sheen realize that he had started, unsurely and with faltering steps, on a spiritual journey. "It was a dark night for my soul," he said. "We all go through that, you know, that dark night of the soul, when we have to face ourselves and accept ourselves and learn to love ourselves."

During that difficult period of his life, Sheen was professional enough to keep making movies. Two of the most interesting were *Blind Ambition*, a movie for television aired in 1979, and *The Little Girl Who Lived Down the Lane*, a theatrical picture released that same year. For his role as John Dean, an advisor to President Nixon during the Watergate scandal and the author of a book called *Blind Ambition*, Sheen was briefly nominated for an Emmy. Of course, he politely insisted that his name be withdrawn from the competition.

During this troubled period in his life, Martin Sheen's children were still going to school. But it wasn't long before his oldest child, Emilio, began his own acting career.

A 1947 photo shows five of the
Estevez boys, from the top: Carlos,
Frank, Alfonso, Martin, and Joe
Martin Sheen's father, Francesco
Estevez (top left), at the age of
sixty-six and his mother, Mary Ann
Phelan Estevez (left), at age
twenty-four

Above: Martin Sheen is fourth from the right in the bottom row of the 1954 freshman class of Chaminade High School.
Below: The cast of the 1955 Chaminade High School Dramatics Club presentation of *Arsenic and Old Lace* included Martin Sheen (seated in the center) as Dr. Einstein.

Some films that feature Martin Sheen (clockwise from top left) are: *The Story of Pretty Boy Floyd, The Catholics* with Trevor Howard, *Judgment in Berlin,* and *The Execution of Private Slovik.*

Martin Sheen and homeless activist Mitch Snyder (above left) pose next to a statue entitled *Third World America* that depicts a homeless family on a steam grate. Martin discusses the need for nuclear disarmament at the University of Minnesota (above right). Martin and Kris Kristofferson (below left) join a group of protesters at the Nevada nuclear test site. Father Daniel Berrigan (below right) and Martin walk to a "Star Wars" protest that resulted in Martin's first arrest for civil disobedience.

Some other films in which Martin Sheen appeared are *Eagle's Wing* *(above left)*, *Apocalypse Now* (above right), and *Blind Ambition* (below, left and right).

Above: A 1969 photograph shows the Estevez children, left to right, Emilio, Ramon, Renee, and Carlos "Charlie."
Below: In the movie *Cadence*, Martin Sheen appeared with his sons Ramon (center) and Charlie (right).

Above: Martin Sheen directing his daughter Renee Estevez in a scene from *Babies Having Babies*. This was the last day of shooting and was called "pajama" day.
Below: Emilio Estevez (left) in *That Was Then . . . This Is Now* and Charlie Sheen (right) in *No Man's Land*

Martin Sheen played a reporter in the film *Gandhi,* and Ben Kingsley starred as Gandhi. Being involved in this film of Gandhi, in India, had a profound effect on Martin.

Chapter 6

A FAMILY AS BIG AS THE WORLD

Emilio Estevez graduated from Santa Monica High School in 1980, a month after his eighteenth birthday. A popular student, he was elected senior prom king that same year, an honor he found to be pretty embarrassing. The oldest of the Sheens' four children, Emilio had insisted on attending public school. He once noted that private schools existed for "parents who have everything except a relationship with their children."

Emilio was a solid high school student, earning mostly A's and B's. Since his earliest days Emilio liked writing. So he took all the creative writing courses his school offered. He was also an avid reader. Math, on the other hand, was a bothersome chore, often producing his lowest grades.

His other interests in high school were primarily sports and theater. A self-confessed beach bum, he spent considerable time hanging out and surfboarding along the Malibu coast. During several summers, the sun bleached his hair white. At sixteen, he became interested in weight lifting and body building. Although he was never very tall—about five feet seven inches as an adult—he quickly built up his muscles. "I looked like a refrigerator with arms," he joked. He also competed in high school wrestling, track, and soccer meets.

As early as the seventh and eighth grades, Emilio often performed in school plays. By his last years at Santa Monica High School, he was a steady and popular participant in the drama department. He also became a professional actor early in his senior year. When he was still seventeen years old, he appeared with his father at a Florida dinner theater in a play called *Mr. Roberts*.

As a high school senior, he wrote an original play about a Vietnam War veteran called *Echoes of an Era*. Emilio acted in the lead role of the drama, and his friend and schoolmate Sean Penn directed it. Of all the plays presented at Santa Monica High that year, *Echoes of an Era* had the most performances and the largest audience.

Emilio's younger brother Ramon was already in his middle years at Santa Monica High School when Emilio graduated in 1980. For years, Ramon had resisted joining Emilio and Carlos in acting projects. He was quiet and somewhat of a loner. But show business still seemed to be in his blood. Throughout his high school years, he developed his talents as a tap dancer. His mother and father attended at least one of his performances and enjoyed it thoroughly.

Ramon also experimented with California's punk rock scene. At one point, he dyed his hair red and blue and wore leather clothes. In a few more years, he also began an acting career as Ramon Sheen, combining his real first name with his father's stage name.

By 1980, Carlos, who calls himself Charlie Sheen, youngest of the three brothers, was just starting a riotous career at Santa Monica High School. In years to come, he missed more than half of his classes. He claimed that he never took a textbook home after his sophomore year. His grades were easy enough to predict. When he did study, it was usually in a last-ditch effort to earn enough C's and D's to be allowed to play on the school baseball team.

Although he also joined football and golf teams, baseball was his true passion. He talked about the sport all the time. For years he planned on trying to become a shortstop for a professional club. Eventually, he settled into his life as a movie star. "If I weren't an actor," he said in 1986, "I would definitely be playing college baseball at this time."

Martin and Janet Sheen's youngest child, Renee, was only thirteen when Emilio graduated from high school in 1980. But three great interests in her early life were already developing: reading, writing, and horseback riding. Her financially secure parents were able to provide her with private riding lessons from the age of seven. She soon developed into an excellent equestrian.

Martin and Janet Sheen both hoped that Emilio would go

on to college after leaving high school. Emilio's father, of course, didn't even finish his senior year. Janet was a college art student for a time, but dropped out soon after she met her husband.

As luck would have it, Emilio landed his first television job soon after he graduated. He played a juvenile delinquent in a movie called *17 and Going Nowhere*, which was finally aired two years later as an ABC Afterschool Special. He quickly moved on to another television movie, *Making the Grade*, which was shown in 1981. Before 1980 was over, he also appeared with his father in a religious program produced by Catholic priests.

With an acting career already in full swing, Emilio thought little more about college. At the age of eighteen, he was about to embark on one of the greatest adventures of his youth, one that he would share with his father. That same project would also mark a turning point in the troubled life of Martin Sheen.

Until his assassination in 1948, the Indian political leader Mohandas Karamchand Gandhi, better known as Mahatma Gandhi, was considered by many to be the world's greatest living hero. Gandhi devoted his life to a nonviolent struggle against political and social unfairness.

Using entirely peaceful forms of protest, he virtually forced British rulers to give up control of his native India in

1947. He used a number of nonviolent demonstrations, including long personal fasts, to stop religious violence between Indian Hindus and Indian Muslims.

By 1960 the English film director Richard Attenborough began making plans to make an epic movie about Gandhi's life. Twenty years later, in 1980, the recently knighted Sir Richard Attenborough finally began production of *Gandhi*. Impressed by Martin Sheen's work, the director offered the actor the role of an American journalist who becomes a follower of the Indian leader.

Ten years after he was offered the part, Sheen still remembered his first reaction. "I knew I was going to be changed forever," he said. Still struggling to get his personal life in order, Sheen was afraid to travel to India. But he simply could not turn down a role in such an important motion picture. Besides, it would give him a chance to work with Emilio, who had been hired to work as his stand-in. Movie companies often use stand-ins to allow actors to rest while scenes are being prepared. Stand-ins are sometimes filmed from a distance or from the back. Since Emilio looked a great deal like his father, he was a natural choice.

Early in 1981, Martin and his eighteen-year-old son flew to India. Having already traveled to Mexico and the Philippines, both, like India, poor nations, the elder Sheen had at least an inkling of what was ahead. Nevertheless, both father and son were stunned by their experiences there. In an interview conducted in October 1990, Martin Sheen struggled to find words to describe the event.

"Have you ever been to India?" he asked. "You see, it's difficult to translate that experience because everyone who goes there feels it in different ways. But you cannot not be affected, deeply, to the roots of your being, because you see a whole nation living on the edge of life and death—literally!

"The poverty is horrible. It's HORRIBLE! You can't imagine such poverty," he continued. "And yet the joy and the vibrancy of life is *equally* impressive.

"You witness it. You're a stranger walking through this land. And you see children horribly disfigured and you see them starving. You see them with disease and you see the Third World in its most horrible need.

"And you're white. And so you are instantly recongnizable and instantly seized upon in the streets, in public. You can't escape it.

"In the first couple of weeks, Emilio would dive into the crowds and give away everything. He was just amazed by it. I was afraid. I would go to work, but I wouldn't leave the hotel otherwise. I was terrified. . . . He [Emilio] was terribly impressed by it as well. But I was on a different journey. Man, he was eighteen. I was forty. To me, it was touching my spiritual life. I knew I was going to be changed forever."

Sheen's role in *Gandhi* was a relatively small one. He and Emilio completed their work and returned to the United

States before filming was finished. The movie was released the following year, 1982. It soon swept most of the major Academy Awards, including best picture, best director, best actor (Ben Kingsley as Gandhi), best original screenplay, and best cinematography. Many critics still regard *Gandhi* as one of the finest movies ever made.

All of this, of course, was still ahead when Martin and Emilio returned to the United States. It would be a year or so before theatergoers would be able to see *Gandhi*. But his work in India was already changing Martin Sheen's life.

Back in 1977, soon after he suffered his heart attack in the Philippines, Sheen briefly tried to return to the Catholic church. But the fear that drove him there gradually lessened and he fell away once again. Reborn during a brief period of panic, his Christian faith was not strong enough to continue after his heart condition improved.

Somehow, the impoverished masses of India—people who owned virtually nothing—were able to give him a priceless gift, the gift of renewed faith. In the countless faces of India's pitiful children, he saw his own more fortunate family. From that point on, it was difficult for him to think of any real family smaller than the whole, wide world. After an absence of more than a decade, he returned to the Catholic church for good.

"The experience in India was one I really needed," Sheen said. "That was the final step that pushed me toward coming to grips with my spirituality. . . . The Indian experience really solidified the journey for me. I had to surrender to my need, to address my spiritual need. And rather than coming to the church out of fear, I came back out of love."

Of course, it was a love that requires some explanation. Over the next decade, it led him to more than forty arrests.

Chapter 7

"THEY SHALL TURN THEIR SWORDS INTO PLOWSHARES"

A few months before Martin Sheen traveled to India, a brief antinuclear protest occurred in the United States that would soon have an important influence on his life. Sheen was nowhere near the little Pennsylvania town where the protest was made. But he soon got to know—and love—the protestors who were arrested there.

On September 9, 1980, eight people walked through the unlocked entrance of a General Electric Space Division plant in King of Prussia, Pennsylvania. In the group were two Catholic priests named Father Daniel Berrigan and Father Carl Kabat and a Catholic nun named Sister Ann Montgomery. Among the remaining five was Philip Berrigan, a former priest and the brother of Daniel Berrigan. The Berrigan brothers had organized the group. All eight people were carrying hammers.

As soon as they entered the factory, Sister Montgomery and Father Kabat began talking to a security guard. The other six walked deeper into the building. Seeing what was happening, the guard started to make a telephone call, but Sister Montgomery had her hand on the phone. The guard removed it and made his call. Father Kabat and Sister Montgomery hurried to join the other six.

None of them knew the layout of the plant, but they all knew what they were looking for. As luck would have it ("It was a very graced day," Father Kabat said), they found it immediately. Inside one of the first rooms they looked in were two unarmed Mark 12-A nuclear warheads. Once armed, each of the weapons would have an explosive power twenty-eight times greater than the atomic bomb dropped on Hiroshima, Japan, in 1945. Some American military leaders were planning to put *twelve* of these warheads into the nose cone of a single MX missile.

Father Kabat was the last of the eight to enter the room. When he saw a guard rushing toward the doorway, Kabat knelt down. "It's all right brother," he told the guard, hoping to delay him. Daniel Berrigan and six others were already at work inside the room.

Martin Sheen wasn't there, but he described what happened. "They pounded on the nose cones of two of these MX-12s and poured their blood on them," he said. "Then they held hands and sang hymns and read Scripture until they were arrested."

The group called themselves the "Plowshares Eight." The name was taken from a prophecy in the Bible that states, "in the last days they shall turn their swords into plowshares." The act of hitting the warheads with hammers was both real and symbolic. Symbolically, the protest was meant to show that weapons—the swords of the Bible—could be turned into tools of peace, such as the plows used by farmers at planting time. But real damage was also done to the warheads, and they were unbelievably expensive.

"When the state puts such resources into weapons of destruction," Father Kabat said from a jail cell in 1979, "it's a healthy thing for Christians to be in trouble with the state."

The warheads the Plowshares found in Pennsylvania have never exploded. But in *America* magazine, a Jesuit publication, Father Kabat asked, "How many have they killed already?" Years earlier, the Catholic pope had declared that weapons are killers even if they are not used. The money spent to build them might have been used to feed starving people.

The trial of the Plowshares Eight was held in the Montgomery County Courthouse in Norristown, Pennsylvania. Of the eight defendants, the ones best known to American law officials were the Berrigan brothers and Father Kabat.

In 1968, during the height of the Vietnam War, a group of Catholic priests and lay people led by Phil and Daniel Berrigan poured their own blood on military draft records in Catonsville, Ohio. For that protest and many others, the Berrigan brothers and Father Kabat spent years in prison. More prison years were to come.

The Plowshares decided to defend themselves in court.

Among their legal assistants was Ramsey Clark, attorney general of the United States in 1967. Probably because he was so well known, Daniel Berrigan was allowed to speak for about fifteen minutes during the trial. Others were not given such freedom. Father Kabat asked a juror, "Do you think you should follow your conscience?" Judge Samuel W. Salus II, who was presiding, refused to allow the question.

A number of jurors seemed swayed by the defendants' arguments. In the end, however, Judge Salus gave the jury instructions that made it impossible to find the defendants innocent. Two jurors cried as the guilty verdict was read.

"Those of our group, including my brother Philip, passed considerable time after our trial in Salus's lockup," Daniel Berrigan wrote in *To Dwell in Peace*, his thirty-seventh book. He was released for a time while the case was appealed to a higher court. But Father Berrigan eventually spent even more time in federal prison.

On the back cover of *To Dwell in Peace* is a single sentence written by Martin Sheen in praise of the book. He called it, "A powerful and poetic account of Berrigan's life and work, as well as a prophetic call to go forth in faith striving towards the long promised blessing reserved for the peacemakers."

Father Berrigan was able to enjoy a period of freedom between his stays in Judge Salus's jail and a federal penitentiary. It was during that time in 1981 that he met Martin Sheen in New York City. The two men became friends.

Nine years later, Sheen recalled how they met. "A friend of mine, Emile de Antonio, a very famous documentary filmmaker. . .wanted to do a documentary on these people [the Plowshares]. He started working, doing interviews with them, and going to the trial daily. He asked permission to film in the courtroom but the judge refused. So he got the idea of dramatizing the trial. He got the transcript and he hired actors to play all the members of the court and he got the Plowshares—the eight defendants—to play themselves.

"It is a historic film," Sheen continued. "And you can see it. It was done on tape and we shot it in less than forty-eight hours in New York City in July of 1981. It's called *In the King of Prussia*. I play the judge. That's how I met Dan Berrigan, and Phil, and all the other Plowshares. That was a milestone in my life."

All of this happened soon after Sheen returned from India. The experience there had renewed his Christian faith. Once again, he was ready to go back to the Catholic church, this time to stay. Father Berrigan, a Jesuit, became the priest to whom Sheen confessed his sins. In a few more years, that same priest showed him the express lane to more than forty different jail cells.

It took some time before Sheen's conscience overcame his fear of arrest. In 1985, he visited Father Berrigan and others in the federal penitentiary in Alderson, West Virginia. Not much later, in October of that year, he spoke to a reporter from the *New York Daily News* about his growing concerns. "I don't have the guts to go to jail," he said. But his first arrest for political activism came less than a year later.

In the meantime, he began to speak out against what he felt were unjust policies of the United States government. He also supported others who did the same.

For decades, the United States has given billions of dollars in military aid to El Salvador, a tiny country in Central America. Money and weapons were given to the El Salvadorean government in the hope it could resist a takeover by rebels that U.S. leaders believed were Communists.

Unfortunately, the anti-Communist government of El Salvador was hardly a model of democracy. It was heavily influenced—some say owned—by a group of fourteen or so wealthy Salvadorean families and their friends. A number of these families had made fortunes by growing coffee beans on huge plantations.

Certain members of the El Salvadorean government, military, and ruling families organized groups of hired killers, popularly known as "death squads." Over the years, suspicions were widespread that the death squads murdered more than twenty thousand people. Among the suspected victims were priests, nuns, missionaries, teachers, reporters, farmers, students, and even children. Some of the victims were Americans. Anyone who even hinted at criticism of El Salvador's government was a potential victim.

Some Americans began to think that the United States should not send military aid to a country that tolerated death squads. One of the people who found the courage to speak out was a television actor named Ed Asner. Asner is probably best known for his role as Lou Grant, a newsman introduced on the *Mary Tyler Moore* show and later showcased in a program of his own called *Lou Grant*. Asner also served as president of the Screen Actors Guild.

In late 1981 and early 1982, Asner publicly criticized his country's military support for the government of El Salvador. He soon paid a heavy price for his words. Among the people who criticized Asner was Ronald Reagan, the president of the United States.

"[President] Reagan was attacking Asner from the White House," Martin Sheen recalled. "And he was making his life miserable. Ed had to have LAPD [Los Angeles Police Department] protection on himself and his family because he got so many death threats. I feared for his life. But I also feared for the destruction of our rights to take a stand in honest protest."

Sheen decided to show his support for his fellow actor. He took out paid advertisements in a number of newspapers read by people in the television and motion picture business, including *Daily Variety* and *Hollywood Reporter*. The ad was in the form of a letter that began with the salutation "Dear Ed," and ended with Sheen's signature. Two of the sentences read: "Thank you for accepting the responsibility most of us have conveniently chosen to ignore. I'm proud of your courage and deeply moved by your compassion."

The two actors began working together to raise money to send medical supplies to El Salvador. Before long, Asner's televison show was canceled and Sheen was receiving death threats of his own. At about that time, Martin and Janet began taking precautions with their mail. Whenever a mysterious package arrived at their Malibu home, they submerged it in water in their kitchen sink before opening it. Eight years later, in 1990, Sheen was still paying a price for his own activities in opposition to the death squads of El Salvador.

"Recently, I was supporting a boycott," he said. "I was sending out letters for Neighbor to Neighbor for the boycott of El Salvadorean coffee, which is run by the oligarchy—the fourteen families who support the death squads. We were trying to go after Folgers and Hills Brothers and so forth to get them to ban the coffee from El Salvador. Well, my God, there's an organization in Washington called Defense of the Hemisphere or some crap, I don't know what. But they took after me to boycott and they started a hate campaign, a mail thing, that is still rolling in to Neighbor to Neighbor in San

Francisco. It gets crummy sometimes, but that's one of the risks you have to take.

"You have to have as much compassion as you have conviction," Sheen continued. "They're equally important. You cannot just do something for the sake of doing it. You have to do it because you cannot *not* do it and be yourself, to be honest with yourself, to know yourself. And that upsets a lot of people because you focus attention on issues that are very sensitive. You make people think and make them realize that there is great evil out there and we have to confront it."

During the early 1980s, when Sheen's social and political beliefs were maturing, he continued making movies. One of the best known films from the period is *That Championship Season* (1982). In it, Sheen played a former high school basketball player who meets his coach and some of his old teammates twenty-five years after winning the state championship.

Man, Woman, and Child, released in 1983, is one of Sheen's personal favorites. He portrayed a married California college teacher who suddenly discovers he has a ten-year-old son he never knew. Reviews of the motion picture were mixed, but many critics applauded the fine performances by Sheen and Blythe Danner, who played his wife.

Other films included movie versions of two scary books by Stephen King: *The Dead Zone* (released in 1983) and *Fire-*

starter (1984). Sheen also performed in a number of movies made for television and other theatrical films as well.

In the second half of the 1980s, Martin Sheen continued acting in motion pictures. He also formed his own production company, Sheen-Greenblatt, to produce his own motion pictures. But much of his energy during this period was channeled in an entirely new direction—one guided by his increasing concern over the use of atomic weapons. Some news items from 1986 may help to explain his concerns.

On April 16, the core of a Soviet nuclear reactor in the town of Chernobyl exploded. The lives and future health of tens of thousands of people living near the reactor were threatened. A radioactive cloud was carried by winds all around the world. The catastrophe was created at a plant built to use atomic energy in an entirely peaceful way.

In July, the Environmental Policy Institute reported that radioactive waste was contaminating the soil and groundwater at the Savannah River Plant near Aiken, South Carolina. For the past three decades, the plant had been making material for nuclear bombs.

In October, the U.S. Department of Energy released a secret report about an atomic bomb plant in Richland, Washington. The report showed that, since the 1940s, the huge Hanford nuclear reservation had released surprisingly high amounts of radiation. At the same time, the Department of Energy admitted that hundreds of Americans had been deliberately exposed to radiation without their knowledge by agencies of the U.S. government. It was part of an experiment to see how radioactivity might change people's ability to have children.

In November, the State of Colorado and Union Carbide Corporation agreed on a forty million dollar plan. The money, each side acknowledged, would be used to try to clean up *ten million tons* of radioactive waste left behind in Colorado during development of the world's first atomic bombs.

On December 13, the *New York Times* reported that a third atomic bomb factory, this one in Ohio, was also suffering from major safety problems. On the same day, the *Times* described a number of similarities between the design of the Hanford nuclear reservation in Washington and the Soviet Union's disastrous Chernobyl plant. Throughout that year, and most others, the U.S. government repeatedly rejected plans by other nations to ban the testing of atomic weapons.

On June 27 of the following year, 1987, Richard L. Miller wrote a disturbing article in the *New York Times*. He suggested that people in southwestern Utah were already dying because of U.S. atomic bomb tests made in the area between the years 1951 and 1971. He stated that thyroid cancer there was eight times the national average. Bone cancer rates, Miller claimed, were twelve times higher.

Not all of this news had been made public yet when Martin Sheen decided to risk arrest by protesting against nuclear weapons. For years, Daniel Berrigan and many other people had been holding demonstrations at the Riverside Research Institute in New York City. The institute was studying ways to build President Ronald Reagan's Strategic Defense Initiative ("Star Wars") system. It also studied many aspects of American military's nuclear arms policy.

For about five years, Sheen and Father Berrigan had discussed Martin's growing concern over U.S. nuclearism. In the summer of 1986, the priest and the actor agreed that the time had come.

On June 20, 1986, Martin Sheen joined a group of other protestors at the Riverside Research headquarters. He crossed a line created to keep picketers out of the facility and was promptly arrested for trespassing.

"It was time for me to declare myself," Sheen said. "It was one of the happiest days of my life, if not *the* happiest, because I was finally free."

Chapter 8

A STRUGGLING ACTOR ONCE MORE

In January 1987, Martin Sheen appeared on a nationally televised talk show. During the interview, he mentioned his concerns about the U.S. government's policy of building and testing atomic weapons. He also talked about a huge, 1,350-square-mile test site in Nevada where nuclear bombs were exploded frequently. The federal land was just sixty-five miles northwest of the city of Las Vegas.

"I had mentioned during an interview on one of the morning talk shows," he said, "that I intended to go to the test site on a particular day and to be arrested, and if I was not in jail some few days later, I intended to return and do the same thing."

At the time he gave the television interview, Sheen had already been arrested once at the Nevada Test Site. On September 30, 1986, about 500 medical doctors and other activists had demonstrated there. Among the 139 people arrested was the well-known Cornell University astronomer Carl Sagan. The event was sponsored by the 50,000-member American Public Health Association. Sheen appeared at the next major rally, which was held on November 17. He was arrested crossing a fence between the federal land and a road. A total of 58 other people were arrested as well.

January 27, 1987 was the day that marked the 36th anniversary of the first atomic test at the Nevada Test Site. On that anniversary, more than two hundred protestors appeared at the location, including Martin and Janet Sheen. During the demonstration, one woman knelt down in front of a bus carrying government workers to the test site. She opened a baby bottle and poured red fluid on the ground. "This is the blood of the future!" she cried as police carried her away. "This is the blood of our children!"

A total of seventy-two arrests were made at the site that day. Most protestors were arrested as they were attempting to block buses and cars from entering the federal grounds. Others were taken into custody when they crossed over a fence. Martin Sheen was arrested also, but he wasn't with either group of protestors.

"I never got to the test site," he explained. "I was thousands of feet away in the parking area. . . . My wife and I had just arrived, and we joined a prayer group and I was arrested." It was an odd situation. Although he had not yet broken a law, Sheen was taken to a Nevada jail.

Karen Gray, clerk of the Nye County Justice Court, said that Sheen was charged with threatening to commit a crime against a person or property. She also indicated that an arrest warrant had been issued soon after his appearance on the television program.

The Nevada law under which Sheen was arrested was explained to an Associated Press reporter by Jim Boyer, a spokesman for the U.S. Department of Energy. Boyer said that anyone who threatens to commit a crime in Nevada and then goes to the scene can be arrested and held on a five thousand dollar bond.

"It's called a peace bond," Sheen explained in 1990. "That's what I was arrested on. In other words, it was to guarantee the community that I would not damage property or break the law as I said I was going to do on national television. It's a pretty interesting law. It was originally on the books to keep husbands from beating up their wives or children or beating up someone in the community. Do you know what I mean? It was something very simple like that but they used it on me politically."

Sheen felt it was important to understand that the Nevada law had been used against him improperly. He tried to explain the original intent of the law very clearly. "Let's say I'm an irate husband and I'm drunk on Saturday night and I threaten my wife," he said. "My wife can call the authorities and the authorities can come and arrest me because I am a threat to my wife. They can keep me in jail on a five thousand dollar bond until I come to my senses or do six months in jail if I don't."

The law, Sheen believed, was never intended to be used to stop political demonstrations before they even took place.

Although it took about two years, he eventually won his case in the Nevada Supreme Court. Helping to defend him were former U.S. attorney general Ramsey Clark and lawyers for the American Civil Liberties Union. In the meantime, the actor posted bond and was released from the Nevada jail a few hours after his arrest. But he was not out of the lockup for long.

Just as he said on television, he returned to the Nevada Nuclear Test Site nine days later. The U.S. government had planned to explode its first nuclear device of the year on February 5, 1987. Approximately 2,000 demonstrators arrived at the site in the morning to protest the event. Among the 438 people arrested were Martin Sheen and two other actors, Kris Kristofferson and Robert Blake, and astronomer Carl Sagan. Six Democratic members of the U.S. Congress, including Representative Pat Schroeder of Colorado, were also at the rally, as were Owen Chamberlain, winner of the 1959 Nobel Prize for Physics and Hugh DeWitt, a physicist at the Lawrence Livermore Laboratory in California. After kneeling in prayer with Kristofferson and a number of others, Sheen was arrested for trying to enter the test site grounds.

Nine months later, in November 1987, he was arrested once again at the test site, along with about two hundred other protestors. The sponsor of this rally was the Catholic Worker, the same organization that had fed Sheen hot meals during his early years in New York City.

Earlier in the same year, Sheen held a press conference to publicize a new movie called *The Believers*. One of the reporters who recorded his talk was working for the *Sentinel*, a newspaper headquartered in Santa Cruz, California. "When I go on demonstrations or commit civil disobedience," the *Sentinel* quoted Sheen, "I do it with a profound sense of spirituality. I pray—I don't know what else to do.

"I feel my job is to call attention," he continued, "to try and raise consciousness on this important issue, the nuclear arms race. We are, in effect, practicing a state religion: nuclearism. . . . The weapons have become the gods of our idolatry. This faith teaches us to have faith in the weapons to secure our future. We've accepted the weapons as our personal saviors and we tithe in this religion through our tax dollars." He went on to ask, "How can you spend $200 million a day on defense when people are dying of starvation?"

Early in 1988, Sheen appeared in Tucson, Arizona, for a dinner to raise funds for children wounded in U.S.-backed warfare in Nicaragua. In his speech, recorded in the February 9 edition of the *Tucson Citizen*, he made clear his belief that the American defense budget was damaging America itself.

"We're a nation of war makers," Sheen claimed. "We do it better than anybody else. We do it so well, we can't do anything else. Look around—the best electronic equipment is foreign-made, the best automobiles are foreign-made, the best televisions are foreign-made.

"All we can make are bombs and delivery systems," he continued. "That's where we're financed; that's where we're fed; that's where we're encouraged—and that's where we fail. The money to support that machine, $200 million a day, makes it impossible for us to look after our own people, to create jobs and industry that's civilian-oriented—such as making cars and televisions."

Long before he made his speech in Tucson, Sheen was convinced that many of the problems faced by poor and homeless people in America were worsened by the country's fabulously expensive defense budget. By the spring of 1986, he was already at work on a television movie about homeless people and about one individual who cared for them. The individual's name was Mitch Snyder.

Born to Jewish parents in Brooklyn in 1943, Snyder was once a homeless person himself. His father abandoned his family when Mitch was nine and died a few years later. Mitch himself had a very troubled childhood. He dropped out of high school when he was fifteen. During the next year, he was arrested more than a dozen times. After a period spent moving through a long list of different jobs, he eventually settled down. He married a woman named Ellen and had two children. And then one day he simply vanished, abandoning his wife and two boys.

Snyder turned up sometime later in Las Vegas, where he was arrested in 1970 for using a stolen credit card to rent a car. He was eventually sent to a federal penitentiary in Danbury, Connecticut. There, he met Daniel and Phil Berrigan. The Berrigan brothers were in jail for their activities opposing the Vietnam War. It was still years before the two men became involved in the Plowshares movement.

Snyder asked Phil Berrigan for help in coming to terms with his tormented life. Starting with the gospel of Matthew, Phil began leading him in a study of the teachings of Jesus. Before long, Snyder became a devout Catholic. Father Daniel Berrigan baptized and confirmed him while all three men were still in the Danbury prison.

Released from jail in the summer of 1972, Snyder soon joined an organization called the Community for Creative Non-Violence (CCNV). The CCNV had been created just two years earlier by a Catholic priest of the Paulist order, Father Ed Guinan. When the CCNV opened up its first soup kitchen to feed poor people in the fall of 1972, Mother Teresa of India was on hand to help serve.

By the late 1970s, Snyder turned his attention to homeless people in America. During the 1980s, the number of people living on the streets of American cities increased dramatically. In 1984, Snyder began a long hunger strike to get the U.S. government to turn over an empty building to the

CCNV to use as a shelter. It was a tactic he had used before.

Even the radical Berrigan brothers felt Snyder went too far. Threatening to kill himself to get his way, Phil suggested, was much like extortion. After all, Snyder was using his fast to obtain without charge a huge building for a shelter that he would direct and use as his own living quarters.

Many people, including Gandhi and the American labor leader Cesar Chavez, used hunger strikes to call attention to social issues. Snyder did the same, but, unlike Gandhi and Chavez, he also seemed to benefit a bit from the demands he made. At the same time, his fasts were hardly an example of the nonviolent protests the Berrigans believed in. Nevertheless, it was impossible to doubt Snyder's convictions. "I think he loved the poor in a way that I've never seen them loved by any other person," Phil said in the November 1990 edition of *Vanity Fair*.

Snyder's hunger strike continued into the final days of the presidential election campaign of 1984. On November 4, the CBS news program *60 Minutes* featured a story on Snyder. Somewhat incorrectly, Mike Wallace compared Snyder to Gandhi, Martin Luther King, Jr., and Mother Teresa. The program noted that he was near death.

The very same evening that the *60 Minutes* show aired, President Ronald Reagan issued an order aboard Air Force One granting Snyder his shelter. To this day, that sanctuary for the homeless provides beds, food, and medical treatment for more than a thousand people in Washington, D.C. every night. It is the largest shelter in America.

While Mitch Snyder was regaining his strength in a Washington hospital, he became a national celebrity. Movie producers began a bidding war to get the rights to his life story. A man named Chuck Fries was the eventual winner. His television movie *Samaritan: The Mitch Snyder Story* featured Martin Sheen in the title role.

While he was working with Snyder, Sheen learned many details about the difficult lives street people lead. He discovered that, in the cold months of winter, the homeless often gathered over grates set into streets and sidewalks. Those grates allowed steam from underground tunnels and subway passages to escape into the air. The steam gave much needed warmth to those huddled above.

With Snyder, Sheen was arrested one night trying to keep the police from closing a subway entrance used by the homeless. It gave Sheen an idea for an event he called The Grate American Celebrity Sleepout.

"It was an idea I came up with while I was in jail one night with Mitch Snyder," Sheen said. "We had been arrested for trying to keep a subway entrance open so that the homeless could get some residual heat from the subway tunnel. . . . The night that I spent in the D.C. lockup with Mitch we were talking much of the night and thinking of some of the things we could do to draw attention to the horrible plight of the poor in the streets. And I came up with this idea of the Grate American Celebrity Sleepout.

"I organized it as best I could," he continued. "I am not a good organizer. I took out a couple of ads in the trade papers, *Daily Variety* and *Hollywood Reporter*. I called a lot of people, a lot of celebrities that I didn't know personally but who I thought might be interested. Nearly everyone was sympathetic but very few celebrities actually showed up. The ones that did made a tremendous impression. Dennis Quaid was one of them." Brian Dennehy was another, along with a daytime television actor named Grant Cramer.

On the chilly night of March 4, 1987, a handful of actors huddled over two steam grates in front of the Library of Congress. Joining them were a number of Congressmen, including the late Mickey Leland of Texas, John Conyers of Michigan, and several members of the Kennedy family. Two of the Kennedys had performed months of volunteer work at Snyder's shelter.

Sheen had sponsored the entire event in the hope of getting the U.S. Congress to pass a bill to help homeless people. "By morning," a *New York Times* reporter noted, "he was pale and shivering."

Sheen and Snyder were arrested again in a demonstration in 1988.

Despite the *60 Minutes* report by Mike Wallace, Mitch Snyder was not a saint, although he was certainly dedicated.

He spent the last years of his life living in the CCNV shelter at Second and D streets in Washington. There he committed suicide. His body was found, hanging from a heavy electrical cord, on the afternoon of July 5, 1990.

Throughout 1989 and 1990, Martin Sheen continued making movies and continued getting arrested. In 1989, the Malibu Chamber of Commerce named him Honorary Mayor of Malibu. Sheen immediately declared his hometown a nuclear-free homeless sanctuary. When some business leaders expressed alarm, Honorary Mayor Sheen proclaimed Malibu a free-speech zone.

As a politician, he quickly discovered that controversy carries a price. "I was dismissed from command, apparently," the ex-honorary mayor noted.

Even before his fall from power, the conservative editors of the conservative *Chicago Tribune* observed the situation in Malibu with something close to panic. Under the heading, "Malibu does not rest easy these days," the editors expressed their concerns. "Boy, that Martin Sheen is a card," the May 27, 1989 editorial began. It generally went downhill from there.

On the other hand, the actor has found that supporting controversial causes can sometimes lead to unexpected benefits. One, he recalled, came in 1988, when he was backing a hunger strike by the American labor leader Cesar

Chavez. Chavez has devoted much of his life to helping desperately poor migrant farm workers in the southwestern United States. By helping Cesar Chavez, Sheen found the opportunity to quit smoking cigarettes, a life-long habit that he had found impossible to quit for long.

"I was supporting Cesar Chavez for the Fast for Life in 1988," Sheen said two years later. "My son and I joined a group of people supporting him. I had a chance to meet him, and I was deeply moved in his presence. He was along about the twenty-third day of his fast, and I made a vow to myself that I would stop smoking as long as he stopped eating. He went thirty-five days without eating. So I went thirty-five days without smoking."

Sheen had decided that he would smoke again on the thirty-sixth day. But when the time arrived, he was able to resist the temptation. "Then I decided that I would go to thirty-seven and so forth," he said. "So tomorrow is [always] the thirty-sixth day for me. That was on August 14, 1988. I still count the days. I miss it terribly. I don't drink or smoke anymore. At least not today. Maybe tomorrow, but not today."

Chapter 9

EMILIO AND CHARLIE

During the 1980s, Emilio Estevez and Charlie Sheen appeared in a number of hit movies. "My sons are far and away bigger draws than I've ever been," Martin said proudly in the *Orange County Register*. "But I wouldn't want their lives," he continued. "They can't even walk down the street or carry on a conversation in public without a whole to-do."

During the same discussion, the father admitted that he was at a loss to explain the success of his four acting children, especially Emilio and Charlie. "I promise you," he said, "I had nothing whatsoever to do with it. They came along with me on location when they were little, but I never encouraged them. No one is more surprised by their involvement and more stunned by their success."

At a press conference held in August 1988 to promote *Young Guns*, Charlie was asked if his father ever gave him any advice. "Yes," Charlie responded. "Stay out of the business." Not even one of Martin Sheen's four children followed that suggestion.

Emilio was the first to succeed in motion pictures. Of course, while his big brother was gaining experience in movies, Charlie was picking up one poor grade after another at Santa Monica High School. For awhile, he seemed to resent Emilio's success.

"He was making movies and was very successful at a young age, while I was having trouble with high school," Charlie told the *San Francisco Chronicle* in August 1988. A dose of stardom for himself seemed to be all the medicine Charlie needed. "But now," he added, "as professional peers, we get along great. We have so much respect for each other."

Emilio appeared on three television programs right out of high school. At around the same time, it became clear that he had inherited some of his father's political views. He risked jail by refusing to register for the draft in 1980.

Soon after he returned from India in 1981, Emilio devoted considerable time to making movie adaptations of novels by S.E. Hinton. Although not widely read by adults, four novels by a very young writer named Susan Hinton were extremely popular with teenagers. For the most part, her books dealt with troubled adolescents living in Oklahoma during the 1960s. In 1981, Emilio tried out for roles in two movies based on Hinton novels: *Tex* and *The Outsiders*. He won parts in both films, although work on *The Outsiders* was not scheduled to begin for some time.

Emilio became interested in S.E. Hinton's books. He read all four, including the two not yet optioned for the movies: *Rumble Fish* and *That Was Then, This Is Now*. With his friend Tom Cruise, he raised money to buy a film option for

That Was Then, This Is Now. The option gave him the legal right to make a movie based on the book, but that right would expire in just two or three years. When he wasn't acting, Emilio worked on a screenplay to retell Hinton's story.

Tex, the first film made from a Hinton book, was shot in Oklahoma in late 1981. Emilio's role was a relatively small one. He played the best friend of a character portrayed by Matt Dillon.

When he returned to California, Emilio decided it was time to move out of his parent's house. He didn't go far, though, soon settling in Santa Monica, just a short drive from Malibu.

During 1982, he played in two television productions: an episode of Steven Spielberg's *Amazing Stories* and a movie called *In the Custody of Strangers.* The movie cast included Jane Alexander and Martin Sheen. Emilio told *Seventeen* magazine that working with his father was "terrific. Although a couple of times," he added, "I felt like I had two directors—he didn't tell me what to do, just gave me little suggestions."

Production on *The Outsiders* began in late 1982. The movie was directed by Francis Ford Coppola, the same man who directed Martin Sheen in *Apocalypse Now* just a few years earlier. It was released in 1983 to generally poor reviews. But Coppola and the young actors who appeared in it, including Emilio Estevez, did not make the movie for reviews. Most young people who saw it thoroughly enjoyed *The Outsiders*.

Unfortunately, Emilio had a problem as soon as production on the movie was completed. He couldn't find work for nearly half a year. A similar problem had occurred after filming of *In the Custody of Strangers*. His bad luck continued as he tried unsuccessfully to interest studios and producers in his screenplay for *That Was Then, This Is Now*.

His first big break finally came in a strange little movie called *Repo Man*. Emilio was given a starring role in the film, along with veteran Hollywood actor Harry Dean Stanton. Partly financed by ex-Monkee Michael Nesmith, *Repo Man* is a bizarre comedy about a group of men who repossess automobiles for a living. Emilio played Otto—a newcomer just learning the business—as a punky adolescent. At least in part, he used his younger brother Ramon as a model.

A bigger break came early in 1984, when director John Hughes selected Emilio to join a group of four other young actors who played high school students sent to Saturday detention class. The movie was called *The Breakfast Club.* When it was released in 1985, it became an overwhelming critical and box-office success.

During the year 1985, Emilio Estevez clearly became a Hollywood superstar. *The Breakfast Club* was probably the major cause for his fame. But there were other reasons as well. In that same year, he finally succeeded in bringing out his film version of S.E. Hinton's novel.

It almost didn't happen. In 1984, his option on *That Was Then, This Is Now* expired, and Emilio was unable to raise the several thousand dollars needed to renew it. After yet another false start, he finally began working with a director named Christopher Cain. By the summer of 1984, Emilio had rewritten his screenplay yet again.

Finally, it was in a condition that was good enough to film. Rights were purchased once again, and the movie went into production in July. Emilio had the starring role, and received credit as screenwriter. He should have been listed as executive producer as well, but he was afraid to list his name too many times in the credits.

With a slight change in punctuation, *That Was Then . . . This Is Now* was released late in 1985. As they were for other movies based on Hinton books, the critics were generally unkind to Emilio's movie. Once again, however, most failed to understand the emotional impact the story had on teenagers. *That Was Then . . . This Is Now* was a mild box-office success, earning nearly eight million dollars in the first month after its release.

Critics panned *St. Elmo's Fire*, which also was released in 1985 and also starred Emilio Estevez, among a number of other young actors and actresses. The film was about a group of young men and women who had recently graduated from college. Although the script was not particularly good, audiences seemed fascinated by the ensemble of players, which included many of the hottest young actors in Hollywood. Appearing with Estevez were Rob Lowe, Demi Moore, Judd Nelson, Andrew McCarthy, Mare Winningham, and Ally Sheedy.

In the June 10, 1985 edition of *New York* magazine, David Blum wrote an article entitled "Hollywood's Brat Pack." Blum suggested that Emilio was the "unofficial president" of a group of young actors that included Tom Cruise, Rob Lowe, Judd Nelson, Timothy Hutton, Matt Dillon, Nicholas Cage, Sean Penn, Matthew Broderick, and Matthew Modine. All the actors were in their early twenties, Blum pointed out, none had graduated from college, and none paid any dues learning the acting craft in obscurity (as Martin Sheen had done in New York City).

The point of Blum's article seemed to be that young movie stars were capable of acting just as dumb as most other young people. He included a few embarrassing stories about the majority of his "Brat Pack" actors. Some of the young stars had cooperated with Blum as he researched his article. They now felt betrayed by the modestly embarrassing story. Although Emilio clearly came off as one of the most likable of the young actors, he was quickly labeled a charter member of "Hollywood's Brat Pack" anyway.

Had Blum written his article a few years later, he certainly would have included Charlie Sheen in his club. At the time the story came out, however, Charlie was just beginning to make his mark as an actor.

In 1983, Charlie was finishing his undistinguished career at Santa Monica High School. During his senior year, he still planned on becoming a professional baseball player. The Santa Monica baseball team was particularly strong that season. In a game of national significance, the team was scheduled to play the top-ranked team in California.

"I was either going to pitch or play shortstop—it was to be the biggest game of my life—but then the dean called me in and said I was off the team," Charlie told *Seventeen* magazine. He had earned a failing grade in English, and the big game was set for the very next day. "I took it to the principal," Charlie continued, "but didn't even get my first word out before he said, 'There's no way you're going to put a uniform on,' and I was blown away!"

Charlie left the high school building in a rage. Outside, he picked up a rock and aimed it at a window in the principal's office. As luck would have it, the rock sailed through the only open window on his side of the building. He returned to the school only one more time. "I went to graduation wearing dark sunglasses and a suit," he said, "looking like a Secret Service agent."

As soon as Charlie was out of high school, he gave up his

dream of becoming a baseball player. Instead, he began visiting film producers and directors, hoping to follow in Emilio's footsteps. Before the summer was over, he had landed a job. Unfortunately, it was in a doomed project for a film called *Grizzly II: The Predator.*

Other roles came quickly. In *Red Dawn* (1984), Charlie played a young man who is killed by Russian soldiers invading the United States. Martin Sheen urged him not to take a part in the far-fetched movie. The father felt that it stirred up militaristic passions for the Cold War between the United States and the Soviet Union. (In late November 1990, leaders from the United States, the Soviet Union, and other nations officially declared the Cold War over.)

During the next two years, Charlie's career shifted into high gear. With roles in *Lucas* (1985), and *The Wrath, Ferris Bueller's Day Off*, and *Boys Next Door*, all released in 1986, he was quickly gaining fame. But one more movie from that same year made him a star. That movie, *Platoon*, was about the Vietnam War, the same subject that elevated his father to superstar status just seven years earlier.

Director Oliver Stone spent years trying to raise the money to make *Platoon*. A veteran of the Vietnam War himself, Stone had angry memories about what he felt was an unjust conflict. When he finally got the chance, he focused all his brooding energy into the making of the movie. Warned that Charlie Sheen was a troublemaker and a drinker, Stone hired him anyway for the starring role. Charlie didn't let him down. *Platoon* was a box-office smash, eventually winning three Academy Awards, including best picture and best director.

At the age of twenty-one, Charlie Sheen had arrived. He soon moved out of his parent's home but, like Emilio, he didn't go far. He bought a house along the Pacific Ocean just a short drive from his parent's house.

Of course, the glare of publicity fell on Charlie as it already had on Emilio. It was soon revealed that both brothers had a child with women they did not marry. Even before the story got out, however, Martin and Janet set a wonderful example for both of them. They supported their grandchildren financially, even paying to house the young mothers in comfortable circumstances. Martin frequently expressed his love for all his children. At the same time, he admitted how sorry he was that Emilio and Charlie were forced to make the mistakes of their youth so publicly.

In 1986, the same year that Charlie became a superstar, Emilio starred with Demi Moore in a movie called *Wisdom*. The film was about a pair of contemporary Robin Hoods who rob banks and destroy financial records to help farmers in danger of losing their land. It earned a fair share of bad reviews, but it also gave Emilio the chance to act as his own screenwriter and director.

Charlie got the opportunity to work with his father in

Wall Street (1987), directed, once again, by Oliver Stone. *Wall Street*, like *Platoon*, had a serious message. The film showed how greedy New York wheeler-dealers nearly destroyed a little airline company in order to make quick money.

Both brothers had major roles in *Young Guns*, a Western released the following year. Emilio appeared in the sequel, *Young Guns II* (1990). Of the three other 1988 movies that Charlie Sheen made, the best was probably *Eight Men Out*, directed by John Sayles. The film told the true story of how eight Chicago White Sox players purposefully lost the 1919 World Series. The movie actually succeeded in explaining why superb athletes would chose to throw a championship series. Because the film had a limited budget and he admired John Sayles, Charlie agreed to work for less money than he was normally making.

Even as a movie star, Charlie enjoyed considerable success as a baseball player. He played a pitcher in a well-liked 1989 baseball comedy called *Major League*. During the filming, his fastball was clocked at 82 miles per hour.

That same year, Emilio and his father were involved in a deadly serious project. For some time, Martin had been trying to make a television movie about Mercury Camp, Nevada. There, in the 1950s, American soldiers were deliberately exposed to levels of radiation from atomic bombs that some scientists consider dangerous. ABC, NBC, and CBS all rejected the project because they considered it too controversial. But TNT, a cable network owned by Atlanta's Ted Turner, finally agreed to back it.

Nightbreaker, the two-hour film about Mercury Camp, premiered on TNT on March 8, 1989. Martin Sheen was one of the executive producers. His business partner, William Greenblatt, was producer. In the movie, Martin and Emilio both played a researcher named Alexander Brown at different times in the fictional character's life.

"The telefilm is vivid and dedicated," wrote a reviewer for *Variety* magazine, "and the production an admirable achievement. A scene in which pigs are roasted stands out as a powerful statement—and graphically illustrates the point that corruption and contempt for others can come with power in the the wrong hands."

Renee and Janet and Martin Sheen met Pope John Paul II at the Vatican in 1991.

Chapter 10

MOVING ON

By late October 1990, when Martin Sheen talked at length about his life for this book, things were moving along rapidly in his own career and in the careers of his kids. At the time, Emilio was busy writing one movie and preparing to act in another. Charlie's latest film, *The Rookie*, a police drama costarring Clint Eastwood, was being shipped to theaters across the nation for a December release.

At about the same time, video rental stores were just receiving *Men at Work*, a movie shown in theaters in 1989, which featured both Emilio and Charlie. *Beyond the Stars*, in which Martin portrayed a former astronaut, was making its debut on Home Box Office.

During his talk, Martin Sheen expressed optimism for a new film, called *Cadence*, scheduled for general release in early 1991. He directed it, and appears in it along with Emilio, Charlie, and Ramon. The film is set in 1965 and is about a young G.I. who gets in trouble with the army. "It's a wonderful little film," Martin said. "It really is. I say 'little' with love, you know. It cost five million. It's a very special film to me and its the best thing that Charlie has ever done by far."

Near the end of the interview, Sheen was asked if he ever

became discouraged. After all, only a minority of Americans seem to believe that their country's policies on nuclear weapons, foreign affairs, and poor people need to be changed.

"As long as one person believes it, that's hope to me," he answered. "I'm a very, very optimistic person. I live by hope, faith, and love. I don't think you can separate them."

Near the beginning of the talk, and again at the very end, Sheen expressed surprise that he was to be the subject of a book for young people. He also made it clear that he hoped some students would consider carefully his sometimes unpopular views.

"You know," he said, "when I was a boy I used to spend the study hours in the library reading biographies. I used to love to read biographies about people I admired, who went through struggles and all. If this would reach some kid somewhere and would have some meaning, well, that would be a real gift. . . ."

APPENDIX

STAGE APPEARANCES OF MARTIN SHEEN

The Connection (1959)
Never Live Over a Pretzel Factory (1964)
The Subject Was Roses (1964-1966)
The Wicked Crooks (1967)
Hamlet (1967)
Romeo and Juliet (1968)

Hello and Goodbye (1969)
The Happiness Cage (1970)
Death of a Salesman (1975)
Mr. Roberts (1979)
Julius Caesar (1988)

FILM APPEARANCES OF MARTIN SHEEN

The Incident (1967)
The Subject Was Roses (1968)
Catch-22 (1970)
No Drums, No Bugles (1971)
Rage (1972)
Pickup on 101 (1972)
Badlands (1973)
The Legend of Earl Durand (1974)
Cassandra Crossing (1976)
The Little Girl Who Lives Down the Lane (1977)
Apocalypse Now (1979)
The Final Countdown (1980)
Loophole (1981)
Gandhi (1982)
That Championship Season (1982)
In the King of Prussia (1982)
The Dead Zone (1983)

Man, Woman, and Child (1983)
Enigma (1983)
Eagle's Wing (1983)
No Place to Hide, narrator (1983)
Firestarter (1984)
In the Name of the People, narrator (1984)
Broken Rainbow, narrator (1985)
A State of Emergency (1986)
The Believers (1987)
Wall Street (1987)
Siesta (1987)
Dear America: Letters Home from Vietnam, narrator (1987)
Da (1988)
Judgement in Berlin (1988)
Walking After Midnight (1988)
Cadence (1991)

TELEVISION SPECIALS WITH MARTIN SHEEN

Circus of the Stars (1979)
I Love Liberty (1982)
Actors on Acting (1985)
The Fourth Wise Man (1985)
Spaceflight, narrator (1985)
Quest for the Atocha (1986)
The Blessings of Liberty (1987)
China Odyssey: Empire of the Sun, narrator (1987)

Secrets of the Titanic, narrator (1987)
The Policies of God, narrator (1987)
NBC News Report on America Stressed to Kill (1988)
Ten Blocks on the Camino Real (1988)
The Andersonville Trials (1988)
Montserrat (1988)

TELEVISION APPEARANCES OF MARTIN SHEEN

Regular TV Series
As the World Turns (1967-1968)

TV Movies and Miniseries

The Outer Limits (1962)
My Three Sons (1963)
The Defenders (1963)
Then Came Bronson (1969)
The Subject Was Roses (1969)
Mongo's Back in Town (1971)
Goodbye, Raggedy Ann (1971)
Welcome Home, Johnny Bristol (1972)
Pursuit (1972)
That Certain Summer (1972)
Catholics (1973)
Crime Club (1973)
Letters From Three Lovers (1973)
Message to My Daughter (1973)
The Execution of Private Slovik (1974)
The California Kid (1974)
The Story of Pretty Boy Floyd (1974)
The Missiles of October (1974)
Sweet Hostage (1975)
The Last Survivors (1975)
Taxi! (1978)

Blind Ambition (1979)
The Long Road Home (1980)
Fly Away Home (1981)
In the Custody of Strangers (1982)
Marco Polo (1982)
Choices of the Heart (1983)
The Guardian (1984)
The Atlanta Child Murders (1985)
Consenting Adult (1985)
Out of the Darkness (1985)
News at Eleven (1986)
Samaritan: The Mitch Snyder Story (1986)
Shattered Spirits (1986)
Conspiracy: The Trial of the Chicago 8 (1987)
My Dissident Mom (1987)
The Morning Program (1987)
No Means No (1989)
Beverly Hills Brats (1989)
Nightbreaker (1989)

OTHER TELEVISION WORK OF MARTIN SHEEN

Babies Having Babies,
    director and executive producer (1986)

Beverly Hills Brats,
    director (1989)

OTHER FILM WORK OF MARTIN SHEEN

Judgement in Berlin,
    executive producer (1988)
Da,
    executive producer (1988)

Cadence,
    director (1991)

RELATED WORK OF MARTIN SHEEN

Founder and chairor, Sheen/Greenblatt Productions, 1983
Symphony Pictures

Martin Sheen 1940-

1940 Ramon Estevez is born in Dayton, Ohio, on August 3. Winston Churchill, prime minister of Great Britain, gives his "Blood, Sweat, and Tears" speech as World War II continues. German army enters Paris, France. British forces are evacuated from Dunkirk, Belgium.

1941 Germany invades the Soviet Union. Churchill and Franklin Roosevelt, president of the United States, meet and sign Atlantic Charter. British Royal Air Force bombs Nuremberg, Germany. Japanese bomb Pearl Harbor. U.S. and Britain declare war on Japan. Germany and Italy declare war on U.S. U.S. declares war on Germany and Italy.

1942 U.S. transfers more than 100,000 Japanese-Americans to West Coast internment camps. German army reaches Stalingrad, U.S.S.R. The murder of millions of Jews in gas chambers begins. Mohandas K. Gandhi demands independence of India and is arrested.

1943 London suffers new German bombing attacks. Allied forces in North Africa are placed under General Dwight D. Eisenhower's command. U.S. forces regain islands in Pacific from Japanese. Churchill, Roosevelt, and Joseph Stalin, dictator of U.S.S.R., hold Teheran (Iran) conference. Allied "round-the-clock" bombing of Germany begins.

1944 Heavy air raids on London. D-Day: Allies land on Normandy. French general, Charles de Gaulle, enters liberated Paris. U.S. troops land in Philippines. Franklin Roosevelt is elected for fourth term. Vietnam declares herself independent of France.

1945 Roosevelt dies; Vice-president Harry S. Truman becomes president of the U.S. Italy's Fascist leader, Benito Mussolini, is killed by Italian partisans. German leader, Adolf Hitler, commits suicide. Berlin surrenders to Russians and Germany capitulates. V.E. Day ends war in Europe. Churchill, Truman, and Stalin confer at Potsdam, Germany. U.S. drops atomic bombs on Hiroshima and Nagasaki. Japan surrenders.

1946 United Nations (U.N.) General Assembly holds its first session in London. Churchill gives his "Iron Curtain" speech.

1947 British proposal to divide Palestine is rejected by Arabs and Jews. Question is referred to U.N., which announces plan for partition. India is proclaimed independent and is partitioned into India and Pakistan.

1948 In India, Gandhi is assassinated. Communists begin taking over Eastern Europe. The Jewish state of Israel comes into existence. Truman is elected president of the U.S.

1949 Israel is admitted to the U.N. German Federal Republic comes into being, with Bonn as capital. Apartheid is established in South Africa.

1950 President Truman instructs Atomic Energy Commission to develop hydrogen bomb. Nelson Mandela of South Africa becomes president of African National Congress (ANC) Youth League. Senator Joseph McCarthy of Wisconsin begins "witch-hunt" of Communists in the U.S. North Korea forces invade South Korea, beginning the Korean War.

1952 Anti-British riots erupt in Egypt. King George VI of England dies; he is succeeded by his daughter Queen Elizabeth II. Dwight D. Eisenhower is elected president of the U.S. Mandela is arrested for defying 11:00 P.M. curfew.

1953 Korean War ends. Mandela appears in court as a lawyer. Jonas Salk begins inoculating children with polio vaccine. Concern rises in Europe and America about fallout from radioactive waste.

1954 Colonel Gamel Abdul Nasser seizes power in Egypt. U.S. Supreme Court rules that segregation by color is unconstitutional.

1955 Blacks in Montgomery, Alabama, organize a bus boycott. Raids on the Israeli-Jordanian border increase.

1956 Jordan and Israel accept U.N. truce proposals. Nasser is elected president of Egypt. Nasser seizes Suez Canal; British and French nationals leave Egypt. Eisenhower is reelected president of the U.S.

1957 Ramon Estevez auditions for spot on TV show, *The Rising Generation.* Israeli forces withdraw from Sinai Peninsula and hand over Gaza Strip. U.N. reopens Suez Canal to navigation. U.S. declares that forcing blacks into "separate but equal" public schools is unconstitutional.

1958 Ramon travels to New York after winning grand prize as best performer on *The Rising Generation.* He returns to Dayton but is determined to leave again for New York.

1959 Eighteen-year-old Ramon Estevez goes to New York to look for acting jobs.

1960 Ramon changes his name to Martin Sheen. He and a group of other actors organize a performance company called the Actor's Co-op. Sheen finds work, but not acting, at the Living Theater. Sheen meets an art student, Janet Templeton. John F. Kennedy is elected president of the U.S. The American Heart Association associates higher death rate from heart attacks with smoking of cigarettes. In South Africa, 69 antiapartheid demonstrators are killed and almost 200 are wounded.

1961 Ramon Estevez and Janet Templeton are wed on December 23. Sheen travels to Paris with the Living Theater, official representative of the U.S. at the Theater of Nations Festival. He makes his TV debut with *The Defenders.* The Berlin Wall, separating East Germany and West Germany, is constructed. The Republic of South Africa becomes a nation and Nelson Mandela goes into hiding as he works for the cause of freedom.

1962 Emilio Estevez is born on May 12. U.S. military council established in South Vietnam.

1963 Ramon Estevez is born on August 3. Sheen makes a guest appearance on *East Side, West Side* with George C. Scott. The Reverend Martin Luther King, Jr., gives his "I Have a Dream" speech at the Lincoln Memorial in Washington, D.C. Mandela and 8 others are tried in South Africa for conspiracy. President John F. Kennedy is assassinated. Lyndon B. Johnson becomes president of the U.S.

1964 Martin Sheen makes his Broadway debut in *Never Live Over a Pretzel Factory.* Later that year he is in *The Subject Was Roses.* Together with many show business personalities he organizes a benefit to aid the civil-rights movement. President Johnson pushes for passage of the Civil Rights Bill. Martin Luther King, Jr., wins the Nobel Peace Prize. Nelson Mandela is sentenced to life imprisonment. United States begins bombing of North Vietnam.

1965 Carlos Estevez is born on September 3. There are outbreaks of racial violence in Selma, Alabama. Martin Luther King, Jr., leads 4,000 civil-rights demonstrators in march from Selma to Montgomery. Voting Rights Act signed by President Johnson. Marines are sent to Da Nang, Vietnam.

1966 Mrs. Indira Gandhi becomes prime minister of India. Dr. Michael de Bakey plants plastic arteries leading to an artificial heart that functions through a three-and-a-half-hour valve-replacement operation. Demonstrations against American involvement in Vietnam War occur.

1967 A daughter, Renee, is born to Ramon and Janet Estevez. Martin gets his first role in a theatrical motion picture, *The Incident.* A six-day war between Israel and Arab nations begins. Israeli forces move into Sinai Desert and Jordan, capture old city of Jerusalem, and gain control of Sinai approaches to Suez Canal. In the U.S., 50,000 people demonstrate against Vietnam War. Dr. Christiaan Barnard performs first human heart transplant operation.

1968 Reverend Martin Luther King, Jr., leader of the civil-rights movement and winner of the 1964 Nobel Peace Prize, is assassinated in a Memphis motel. Senator Robert F. Kennedy is assassinated. Tet offensive; North Vietnamese and Viet Cong attack South Vietnamese cities and towns. Richard Nixon is elected president of the U.S.

1969 Sheen works in Mexico on the film *Catch-22*. Hundreds of thousands of Americans demonstrate against the Vietnam War.

1970 In the U.S. student protest against the Vietnam War results in killing of four by National Guard at Kent State University, Ohio; 448 U.S. colleges and universities are closed or on strike.

1971 U.S. bombs Vietcong supply routes in Cambodia and conducts large-scale bombing raids against North Vietnam.

1972 Richard Nixon is reelected president of the U.S. in a near-record landslide. District of Columbia police arrest five men inside Democratic National Headquarters in the Watergate Hotel, beginning the "Watergate Affair."

1973 Sheen goes to Ireland to act in a TV film called *Catholics*. Fighting breaks out in the Middle East between the Arabs and the Israelis. After initial gains the Arabs are pushed back. Arab oil-producing nations move to embargo shipments to the U.S. The cutoff precipitates an energy crisis in the industrialized world. The United States, North and South Vietnam, and the Viet Cong sign a cease-fire agreement; the last U.S. ground troops leave Vietnam.

1974 Sheen does TV special, *The Execution of Private Slovik*. Later that year he plays Robert Kennedy in *The Missiles of October*. The Federal Communications Commission establishes new guidelines to encourage the hiring of blacks and minorities. After marathon negotiating sessions, U.S. Secretary of State Henry Kissinger persuades Syria and Israel to agree to a cease-fire on the Golan Heights. President Nixon is implicated in Watergate scandal. Nixon resigns and Vice-president Gerald R. Ford becomes president.

1975 Sheen works on a number of live stage productions and films for TV. Blacks in South Africa battle armed policemen as waves of rioting and violence against apartheid spread. John Mitchell, John D. Ehrlichman, and H.R. Haldeman—powerful members of the Nixon administration—are convicted and sentenced for their roles in the Watergate break-in. Egypt opens the Suez Canal eight years after it was closed during the Arab-Israeli conflict of 1967.

1976 The U.S. marks the start of its American revolution bicentennial with ceremonies at the Old North Church in Boston. North and South Vietnam are reunited as one country after 22 years of separation. U.S. and U.S.S.R. sign treaty limiting size of underground nuclear explosions. Blacks in South Africa battle armed policemen as waves of violence and rioting against government policies spread. James Earl "Jimmy" Carter is elected president of U.S.

1977 While filming in the Philippines, Martin Sheen suffers a heart attack on March 5. President Carter grants amnesty to almost all the American draft evaders of the Vietnam War era.

1978 Israel Premier Menachem Begin and Egyptian President Anwar Sadat agree on a framework for Mideast peace at Camp David summer talks arranged by U.S. President Jimmy Carter. Shah Mohammed Pahlavi of Iran imposes martial law to put an end to violent antigovernment demonstrations.

1979 Sheen stars in *Apocalypse Now*. The American Embassy is taken hostage by Islamic militants in Iran. Sixty-three Americans are held by militant followers of Iran's Ayatollah Khomeini who demands the return of the former shah, who was undergoing medical treatment in New York.

1980 President Carter breaks relations with Iran after Islamic militants continue to hold American

Embassy employees. Ronald Reagan is elected president, the first candidate since Franklin Roosevelt to defeat an incumbent.

1981   Sheen and Father Daniel Berrigan, an antiwar activist, become friends. On his last day in office, President Carter announces that a deal has been reached for the release of the hostages in Iran. Minutes after the new president's inauguration, the hostages are released after 444 days in captivity. The first official mention of AIDS, auto-immune-disease syndrome, in the U.S. is made by the Centers for Disease Control in Atlanta, Georgia. Anwar Sadat is assassinated by Muslim militants. Sheen stars in *That Championship Season* and *Gandhi*. He takes out ad in *Daily Variety* and *Hollywood Reporter* to support Ed Asner's criticism of U.S. support of the El Salvador government. Israel invades Lebanon in a campaign that will drive Yassir Arafat and his organization, the Palestine Liberation Organization (PLO), from their base in Lebanon and make Syria the power broker there. Dr. Barney Clark becomes the first recipient of a permanent artificial heart, but dies four months later.

1984   President Reagan is reelected president.

1985   Mikhail S. Gorbachev becomes leader of the Soviet Union. Palestinian terrorists seize an Italian cruise ship, the *Achille Lauro*, in the eastern Mediterranean Sea, and kill an American passenger.

1986   Sheen is arrested at Riverside Research headquarters in New York City. A reactor at a Chernobyl nuclear plant in the Soviet Union explodes, leaving a cloud of radioactive debris.

1987   Sheen arranges the Grate American Celebrity Sleepout in Washington, D.C. Sheen is arrested in protests at Nevada Nuclear Test Site.

1988   Sheen raises money for children wounded in U.S.-backed warfare in Nicaragua. George Bush is elected president of the U.S. Rioting breaks out in the Israeli-occupied territory of Gaza after a truck driven by an Israeli kills four people near a Palestinian refugee camp. Unrest spreads to the West Bank. The intifada—or uprising—begins.

1989   Sheen named honorary mayor of Malibu, California. Soviet people, for the first time in 70 years, are given a choice of competing candidates in an election. The winners make up part of the new Congress. Thousands of Chinese students mourn the death of a deposed reformist leader. The protests grow and students camp out in Tiananman Square in Beijing. The Chinese military launches a savage assault on the demonstrators, killing an unknown number and crushing dissent. Communism as a system of government fails in the Soviet Union and Eastern Europe. The Polish government legalizes Solidarity and sets elections.

1990   Iraq annexes Kuwait and provokes a storm of world disapproval and the threat of war. East and West Germany are reunited as the Berlin Wall comes down. The Cold War between the U.S. and the U.S.S.R. comes to a close. Tensions rise within the Soviet Union as many of the republics threaten to break loose. One by one, the Soviet bloc falls apart as Eastern Europe moves toward a market economy. Nelson Mandela, now 71 years old, is released from prison after serving over 27 years.

1991   Sheen directs and appears in a film called *Cadence*. The United States, backed by a coalition of members of the United Nations, goes to war against Iraq after its leader, Saddam Hussein, refuses to withdraw from Kuwait. The Iraqis are driven from Kuwait. Violence erupts when the U.S.S.R. moves to quell rebellion in Lithuania.

INDEX- *Page numbers in boldface type indicate illustrations.*

121

About the Author

Jim Hargrove has worked as a writer and editor for more than ten years. After serving as an editorial director for three Chicago area publishers, he began a career as an independent writer, preparing a series of books for children. He has contributed to works by nearly twenty different publishers. His Childrens Press titles include biographies of Mark Twain, Daniel Boone, Thomas Jefferson, Lyndon B. Johnson, Steven Spielberg, Diego Rivera, Nelson Mandela, Richard Nixon, and Pablo Casals. With his wife and daughter, he lives in a small Illinois town near the Wisconsin border.